Arctic Melting

How Global Warming is Destroying One of the World's Largest Wilderness Areas

Chad Kister

Common Courage Press   Monroe, Maine

ISBN 1-56751-284-4 paper
ISBN 1-56751-285-2 hardcover

ISBN 13 paper: 9781567512847
ISBN 13 hardcover: 9781567512854

Library of Congress Cataloging-in-Publication Data is available on request from the publisher

Common Courage Press
121 Red Barn Road
Monroe, ME 04951
800-497-3207

FAX (207) 525-3068
orders-info@commoncouragepress.com

See our website for e versions of this book.
www.commoncouragepress.com

Printed in Canada
First Printing

Acknowledgments

Thanks to my family: my mother Joanna Kister for all her help and guidance, my father Robert Kister, my brother Scott Kister and his wife, Stella and my new niece, Zoe. Thanks to my grandmother, Bernice Hunsinger and my late grandfather Carl Hunsinger.

Thanks to those who have helped me to continue my writing and public speaking: Harvard Ayers, John Cooper, the Mast General Store, Hanes Boren, Footsloggers, Dick and Eleanor Edgar, Art and Peggy Gish, Ann Bonner, Keith McPencow, Pat Westfall, Erik Dumont and Dan Ritzman. Thanks to Deborah Williams, Guntner Weller, Josefino Comiso, Glen Juday, Bruce Molnia, Pam Miller, Fran Mauer and all the others who took the time for me to interview them.

Thanks to my mentors, Sarah Ortman and Ted Bernard. Thanks to Ralph Izard, Dru Evarts, Tom O'Grady and many more.

Thanks to the Alaska Coalition (www.alaskacoalition-.org). the Alaska Wilderness League (www.alaskawild.org) and the many other organizations working to protect public lands in Alaska. Thanks to Greenpeace (www.greenpeace.org) and the many other organizations working to combat climate change and implement solutions to our suicidal path of no return.

Dedication

This book is dedicated to the thousands of activists and organizations who are working to implement the Kyoto Protocol on all levels from local to global, and other means of reducing greenhouse gas emissions.

A further dedication goes to those who will be inspired through the words of top climate scientists and native peoples to join the rising environmental movement and work to reduce and ultimately stop greenhouse gas emissions while creating a nicer, cleaner, healthier world and sustainable economy.

Through a change to muscle power, mass transit, efficiency, wind, solar and other renewable and ecological sources of energy, we can meet our needs while improving our health and safeguarding the future. It is the moral duty of our day to take the time to learn about this critical issue, and make the changes before it is too late.

Contents

Preface   1

Part One: The Problem   2

Chapter 1: A Change in the Weather   3

Chapter 2: The Big Picture   12

Chapter 3: Traditional Knowledge Less Relevant
        in Changing Climate   16

Chapter 4: Retreat of the Glaciers   26

Chapter 5: The Melting Permafrost   33

Chapter 6: Decreasing Pack Ice   42

Chapter 7: Walrus   51

Chapter 8: The Decline of the Black Guillemots   54

Chapter 9: The Fate of the Polar Bear   57

Chapter 10: Pentagon Calls Climate Change
        More Serious Threat Than Terrorism   62

Chapter 11: Sea Coasts Crumble Into Sea   67

Chapter 12: Kivalina   71

Chapter 13: Shishmaref   74

Chapter 14: Opening the Northwest Passage   79

Chapter 15: Movin' on Up: Animals and Plants
        Migrate North   82

Chapter 16: Locking Horns with Climate Change:
        The Caribou Challenge   88

Chapter 17: Feedback Loops   94

Chapter 18: Chill Out: How Global Warming
        May Make the North Atlantic Cooler   97

Chapter 19: Alaska's Dying Forests   101

Chapter 20: Heat Wave   105

Chapter 21: Vanishing Tundra   114

Chapter 22: Change in Snowfall   116

Chapter 23: Interference with Arctic Oil Exploration   119

Chapter 24: Dire Future   127

Chapter 25: Human-Caused or Natural?   133

Part Two: Solutions   137

Chapter 26: Taking the Heat Off:
   Slowing Climate Change   138

Chapter 27: Efficiency: Reducing Climate Change
   While Helping the Economy   144

Chapter 28: Winds of the Future   148

Chapter 29: Solar Powering the World   159

Part Three: The Arctic Refuge   164

Back Side of the Moon or The Last Great Refuge?   165

About the Author   185

Preface

Major changes are wreaking havoc on the Arctic environment, melting the ice of the Arctic Ocean, melting the permafrost, killing millions of acres of forest, eroding shorelines, crumbling native villages into the sea and disrupting Arctic ecosystems. The extinction of Arctic megafauna like polar bears, walrus and seal is predicted, unless massive changes are made in our energy sources.

I experienced the massive, horrific changes to the Arctic in the summer of 2004 in my journey hundreds of miles down the Porcupine River and through the Arctic Refuge. The tundra was much drier and the landscape far different in just the 13 years since I had backpacked more than 700 miles through the Arctic in 1991. Giant sinkholes caved into the permafrost, riverbanks eroded into the sea and giant foot-wide cracks opened along lake banks, where the permafrost was melting.

The climate changes are being caused mostly by the burning of fossil fuels. This marks the first time in the nearly 5 billion-year history of the Earth that a species has caused such a massive change in the climate of the entire planet.

We not only can, we must make the shift to greater efficiency and solar and wind energy if we are to leave a planet with the diversity of life as we know it to our children. The facts are far too proven by thousands of scientists to ignore. The impacts are far too severe to leave our fate to politicians guided by the interests of the fossil fuel industries that are causing the destruction.

Instead of leaving it at the doom and gloom of our current path, Arctic Melting shows how we can make massive reductions and ultimately eliminate our emissions of greenhouse gases through increasing efficiency in every sector of our economy, and changing entirely to solar and wind generated energy. This does not require new technology or excessive monetary input, but can easily be done using existing technology and economic resources.

Part One

THE PROBLEM

CHAPTER ONE

A Change in the Weather

For the first time in 50 million years, visitors to the North Pole can see something extraordinary: water," reported the San Francisco Chronicle, August 22, 2000.

"Alaska is melting," Knight Ridder reported July 31, 2003. "Glaciers are receding. Permafrost is thawing. Roads are collapsing. Forests are dying. Villages are being forced to move, and animals are being forced to seek new habitats."

The Arctic Climate Impact Assessment team, a group of 300 scientists and indigenous peoples, found that year-round average temperatures have risen by five degrees Fahrenheit in Alaska since the 1960s, and average winter temperatures soared eight degrees in that period. Scientists at the Intergovernmental Panel on Climate Change predict the Earth is expected to warm by 2.5 to 10 degrees Fahrenheit by 2100. The year 2002 was the hottest year in Alaskan history, and the 2001-2002 winter was the second warmest on record, according to the National Climatic Data Center in Asheville, North Carolina, which found that Alaskan temperatures began to rise dramatically in 1976.

Alaska Republican Senator Ted Stevens, who is not known for being a friend of the environment, said "Alaska is harder hit by global climate change than anywhere else in the world," (NYT, 2003). He said that his state has experienced more profound and startling changes from global warming than anywhere else in the world. Roads and power lines are sagging, villages crumbling into the sea, millions of acres of forests are dead, catastrophic fires are sweeping the state and the impacts have a likely possibility of disrupting marine wildlife, Stevens warned.

Anti-environmental governor Frank Murkowski even admitted global warming is real in the state, saying "it seems like winters are coming later and breaking earlier." Scientists report that the increase in freeze-thaw cycles—the number of times that the ground freezes then thaws out each year—will increase avalanches in northern mountainous regions like Alaska.

"During the last decade, record high annual average temperatures were broken at 14 of 38 reporting stations, while record low annual average temperatures were not broken at any of the stations. No record monthly or annual low average temperatures have occurred at weather stations in Alaska for decades" (Knight Ridder, 2003).

The western Arctic is one of the fastest warming regions in the world, warming at a rate of one and a half degrees per decade for the past three decades, several times the global average. Temperatures are up to 25 degrees higher than normal, according to the Christian Science Monitor. Barn swallows have appeared where they never have before and mosquitoes live in areas like Barrow where they never have before.

New York Times Reporter Timothy Egan reported that the average temperature in Alaska has risen by seven degrees in the last 30 years. Climate models predict that temperatures may rise by as much as 18 degrees more this century. In 2002, Barrow experienced its first thunderstorm, an extremely rare weather condition in the Arctic that usually occurs only in warmer climates. Alaskans mowed their lawns in November 2002 and golfed in February 2003.

University of Alaska at Fairbanks Climatologist Guntner Weller said there is no doubt Alaska is experiencing climate change. "We have seen temperature increases which are pretty pronounced," he said. "We also are doing a circum-Arctic study which includes Alaska, Siberia, Canada and Europe. The temperature increases that we have seen are on the order of 4-5 degrees Fahrenheit for the annual mean. In the winter, the temperature increases are about twice as high—8-10 degrees Fahrenheit. So we have seen substantial warming in the winter for the last 30 years.

"So who cares, who gives a damn about Alaska," Weller asked. "We supply a huge amount of fish and oil to the U.S. Prudhoe Bay is a very low-lying area. It is subject to permafrost thawing, flooding with sea level rises and coastal erosion. Erosion is also a problem in the Yukon Delta. Storm surges can sweep far inland and disturb waterfowl.

"I have a bumper sticker 'Alaskans for global warming.' I have lived in Alaska for 35 years. I moved here in 1968, when the winters always had—60-degree temperatures. I tried to pour a bottle of scotch that I had put outside but it was frozen (something remarkable given that 40 percent ethanol alcohol freezes at –50 degrees Fahrenheit). This is something you cannot do anymore, because the temperature has steadily increased in winter. For the first time, there were never even—40-degree temperatures. The winters are much warmer. The difference between 60 and –40 is much different." Though some may think a warmer Alaska a good thing, Weller said, "I think they are glossing over the big picture. On balance I think there are more negative impacts than positive impacts. People should always keep a balanced view on things.

"I'm a climatologist. I have studied polar climates all my life. I worked in Antarctica, and for the last 35 years here in Alaska. I have always been interested in climate changes."

One of the key figures in bringing the awareness of global warming to the media and the masses is Alaska Conservation Foundation Executive Director Deborah Williams. In her previous position, Williams was the special assistant to the Secretary of Interior for Alaska, a presidential appointment. "In essence I was the right hand man in Alaska to Clinton's secretary of the interior, Bruce Babbitt. The only Secretary's office that exists outside Washington DC is in Anchorage Alaska which reflects the fact that so much of the Department of Interior's mandate is in Alaska. Over 50 percent of all the land that the Department of Interior manages is in Alaska. In the mid 1990s, I received a call from the Vice President's office saying that Al Gore was interested in having regional global warming conferences.

"He was asking the Department of Interior's Secretary office in Alaska to take the lead on doing the conference in Alaska. At that point I knew very little about global warming. I understood it scientifically and theoretically but I had not really thought about its impacts on the ground in Alaska.

"It was fortunate that about the same time, Guntner Weller at the University of Alaska at Fairbanks was planning a conference. So I in essence was able to integrate the Vice President's conference into the conference that Guntner Weller already had planned and was scheduling. The only thing we added was some native voices and my attendance.

"This conference took place and I went up, eager to learn more about global warming and anticipating that it would be mostly a series of scientific presentations talking about the theoretical impacts of global warming. In fact what happened is scientist after scientist stood up and talked about their research and how their research led them to conclude that global warming was having a profound, tangible, measurable impact on what they were studying.

"And in each instance these scientists were basically minding their own business, doing their work on phytoplankton or their work on shrubs or their work on permafrost or their work on glaciers or whatever. They were just doing their work and they slammed into the wall of global warming.

"The only way they could explain what they were observing was through profound warming in Alaska. This was quite eye opening for me, and reinforced that not only was global warming theoretically justified but that it was predicted to have and in fact was having profound, measurable adverse impacts in Alaska.

"All of the climate change modeling did predict that Alaska and some other places in the Arctic would experience the impacts of global warming most immediately and most dramatically. And that is what was being observed across the state from every measurable perspective. I did a little more work on global warming, and communicated that to the vice president's office. I discussed it with Secretary Babbitt and others, but in my position with the Department of Interior, there was very little that I could do to have an impact on the global warming decision-making processes.

"When I came over to the Alaska Conservation Foundation, I was interested in getting the word out more clearly about Alaska. I really feel that Alaska and Alaskans have a moral obligation to explain to the nation and the world what kind of real, on-the-ground measurable adverse effects that global warming is having. Most Americans still think that global warming is theoretical and they don't really appreciate that it is real and measurable and adverse to the extent that it is, and already being experienced in Alaska.

"What we have done at the Alaska Conservation Foundation is to try and publicize both through proceedings and with contacts through the media the real adverse effects of global warming in" the largest state in the U.S.

Williams warned that the change from snow and ice to vegetation and water will itself add greatly to the warming of Alaska and the planet. "When the sun hits Alaska and it finds ice and snow, it reflects back and absorbs very little heat. When it finds vegetation and brown dirt or blue water it absorbs more heat and heats the Earth. Crossing that critical tipping point between freezing and not freezing is why you find this extraordinary change.

"There are places where one degree makes a major difference compared to areas where it makes a minor difference. In Alaska that is what you have so that is why you are seeing the results so dramatically.

The Arctic Climate Impact Assessment Council Report released in November, 2004 found that the Arctic is particularly sensitive to warming because its plants and soil hold less water than more temperate environments. Thus, more of the sun's energy is used for heating the surface rather than evaporating water. Other temperature zones shed heat by shipping it north in ocean currents and wind patterns, but the Arctic is the end of the line on the planet.

"This has been interestingly enough a cold winter in Anchorage (2003-2004). But the last five or six winters have brought very warm temperatures. I am a cross-country skier. In the last several years there have been very few opportunities for cross country skiing. This is a human impact on winter sports and activities. In Alaska, last year we had to reroute the Iditarod dog sled race because of the absence of snow and frozen rivers."

"The latest climate-change anomaly involves the famed Iditarod Trail Sled Dog Race," The San Antonio Express News editorial reported March 3, 2003. "Because of an abnormally warm winter and little snowfall, race organizers had to ship in snow for the ceremonial start in Anchorage; ...they also have had to revise the race route.... In the nation's northernmost state, global warming has become something more than political debate."

"All over Alaska, people are asking the same question: 'where's our winter?'" Rachel D'Oro wrote for the Associated Press December 7, 2002. She reported people were water skiing near Anchorage in December and that trees were budding in the same month.

"Just during the 23 years that I have lived up here I have seen extraordinary change in snow conditions and winter temperatures and in how Anchorage defines itself," Williams said. "There are fewer days for skiing and snowmobiling. In Anchorage, our main winter festival is called the fur rendezvous. And the highlight of the fur rendezvous is the world championship sprint dog races. In the last ten years they had to be cancelled four times because of the absence of snow in February in Anchorage."

The Rendezvous began in 1935, as a winter sports tournament designed to bring people together and bolster community spirit. When it has not been cancelled, it lasts nine days with balls, craft shows, a storytelling competition, snow sculptures, ice bowling, oyster-shucking competitions, the Jim Beam Jam, Cabin Fever Bon Spiel, Pioneer Pancake Feed, Frostbite Footrace, Snowshoe Softball where contestants must drink a beer at each base, auto and sled dog races, canine feats of strength, silly games, time-honored traditions and a carnival. Lori Tobias reported in 2003 that in 1979 when she moved to Anchorage she "remembered days bundled in moon boots, parkas, hats and gloves.... This visit I fly into Anchorage from Portland...I'm still carrying my ski jacket and wearing only a fleece vest over my turtleneck and jeans when I step outside the airport."

The world champion sled dog race is a 25-mile loop around Anchorage at speeds of up to 20 miles per hour. This is in contrast to the 1,122-mile Iditarod race that is run over nine days from Anchorage to Nome with up to 16 dogs per team. The 2003 Fur Rendezvous races had to be canceled because of lack of snow, causing it to be the "furless rendezvous" reported Beth Bragg in the Anchorage Daily News, February 21, 2004. Writing about the festival called Fur Rondy, she said, "A Rondy without dogs is like New Years Eve's without a kiss, the Fourth of July without fireworks, a birthday without a cake.... Two times in the previous three winters, a lack of snow prevented the dogs from running. And both years, Fur Rondy just didn't seem like Fur Rondy."

Bragg quoted Willow Alaska musher Mari Wood's reaction to the cancelled races in 2003. "Every dog musher I know was majorly depressed," she said. Wasilla musher Sato Konno moved to Anchorage from Japan to race in the 2002 Rondy. A car accident prevented her from racing in 2002. Then, in 2003 the races were cancelled, "a double whammy for Konno" Bragg reported. The Torchlight Ski Parade and family skate also had to be cancelled.

Along with the warmth has come fights, riots and police brutality at the Fur Rondy. At the 2003 teen dance, fights broke out and police came in with 70 officers, using batons and pepper spray and reportedly threatening teenagers with assault rifles. Teens threw rocks and bottles at police. That was one of the years when many of the winter activities, including the world champion sled dog races had to be cancelled.

"Just a few days ago, ducks floated on little puddles dotting the Delaney Park Strip and umbrellas, not heavy coats, were in demand downtown" reported Zay Hollander in the Anchorage Daily News on February 16, 2003. "It's warm. It's incredible,"

This photo overlooks Arctic Village from Undercloud Mountain. About a hundred years ago, this was the treeline. Now it is spruce forest, with the treeline being on the other side of the Brooks Mountain Range.

Hollander quoted Anchorage resident Gary Stein as saying.

Josh Niva reported February 23, 2003, "Rondy signs hung off light posts and a nearby fur stand fielded modest interest from passers-by, but the street itself was barren. No snow. No dog sleds. No sled dogs...Warm weather and a lack of snow knocked out the world championship races."

Because of the lack of snow and unstable ice around the state, trappers brought in only half as many pelts as they had for the previous years event. Executive director of the rendezvous Mary Pignalberi said "It is a challenge to pull off a winter festival when you have warm weather." Many dog mushers, snow mobilers and cross country skiers complained about the lack of snow reducing or eliminating their favorite sports, and for many of them that was the reason they moved to Alaska.

Nowhere else is the excessive influence of the oil industry more pronounced than in Anchorage, headquarters of some of the biggest culprits of global warming. It is ironic that the Exxon-Mobile dog sled races had to be cancelled because of global warming, as that company is a leader in the global suicidal effort to discredit the sound science of climate change and stall efforts to reduce greenhouse gas emissions such as the Kyoto Protocol.

Beyond the Arctic, climate change is wreaking havoc around the globe. Discover magazine, January, 2004 was headlined "Deadly Extremes: The Weather Outside Was Frightful." It quoted Kenneth Davidson of the World Meteorological Organization as saying average land temperatures for May, 2003 were the highest in recorded history. Discover also reported that the number of reported tornados has doubled in two decades. Davidson said, humanity's "influence is clear: we've increased the amount of greenhouse gases in the atmosphere, and that's exacerbating the warming trend."

CHAPTER TWO

The Big Picture

Scientists can say with much greater certainty that climate change is real in Alaska in large part because of satellite data. "Climatologists have been hindered until the advent of satellite data, where you really have the global coverage of data every day," said Climatologist Dr. Josefino Comiso. "So they are making breakthroughs now all of a sudden with this satellite data. As we get wiser and wiser in introducing some of the complications then we come up with better and better models, and get to the point where we are able to predict what will happen with the Earth's systems."

Comiso also confirmed major increases in temperature in Alaska. "We observe that over the entire Arctic region, North America shows the highest rate of warming, and that includes Alaska. What I figured out as I looked at long-term data sets, looking at surface data or meteorological data from 1900 to the present, the current trend toward warming as we observe from satellite data is about eight times higher than that of the 100-year data set." That is an unprecedented upswing in the rate of temperature change.

"I focus my studies mainly on polar regions. I do polar regions because that is where satellite data can really help. There are only about 20 meteorological stations in the polar region, whereas if you look at England or Germany, or the lower 48 states of the US, you have meteorological stations all over. They have a very good idea already that there is significant warming. I look at satellite data and this really proves that the global climate is warming.

"We are consistent, as I said. It is only with satellite data that we can have a true global picture of the climate. Looking at Alaska, for example, some areas might even be cooling compared to other areas, such as the Bering Sea region. The sea ice has been expanding in the Bering Strait in the winter. Major meteorological systems in Alaska may be different, and if you try to make deductions from one area, you miss the greater picture.

"With all of these complications, even with the green-house effect, it will not be uniform across the Earth, it may be more in some areas than in others. And therefore, the heating of the Earth can be a very complex thing. In Alaska, there is an earlier spring and a later freeze-up. That would be consistent with permafrost melting more and more."

"There are patterns in the atmosphere," Comiso said. "Sometimes you have cyclonic circulation (counter-clockwise) and sometimes you have anti-cyclonic circulation. So part of the years might be these oscillation variability's in the changing climate system. It is getting warmer in the Beaufort Sea, but cooler in the winter in the Bering Sea."

Climatologist Uma Bhatt said that while the Earth's climate varies in a number of different cycles, some within a decade, some multi-decadal, that the input of greenhouse gas emissions clearly has contributed to a sharp increase in temperatures recently.

"The climate varies naturally with natural variability. You need to understand that on a variety of time scales whether it is year-to-year or decadal or multi-decadal. And you need to understand the factors associated with that before you can come out and say x percent of this trend is due to human induced effects," she said.

Bhatt wanted to predict what will happen if global warming causes a decrease in the amount of ice in the sea in the summer time. To find out, she constructed a series of computer models. "The studies that I have done are in Eurasia, I do climate modeling and fix the sea ice conditions based on the extreme years. If you look at the last 20 years, 1995 was a particularly rogue year. There have been some rogue years since then from the time I started but there was very little sea ice during the summertime. I ran some experiments where I specified the sea ice and then I looked at what happens in the atmosphere.

"In the model, we do see an effect on Alaska. And we do see an effect on the North Pacific. What is happening is the storm tracks, where the main precipitation band that goes across the North Pacific and comes into Alaska, ends up getting shifted northward. There is actually less precipitation in the south part of Alaska.

"And then we have also taken sea ice conditions from a CO_2 warming simulation where it is reduced and it doesn't look

This photo of Misty Mountain was taken after the author climbed over it, and down into Ottertail Creek valley, where the picture was taken. Gwich'in elders in Arctic Village said that just a few decades ago, snow remained through the summer on the taller peaks such as Misty Mountain. Now it all melts. Photo by Chad Kister.

that much different than the summer of 1995. We've forced our models with sea ice conditions so we show with very little sea ice what does that do to the climate in the summertime. And we get a very similar answer that the main precipitation in the band that heads across the Pacific and hits mountains in Anchorage and Juneau is reduced because now there is higher precipitation further to the north.

That is potentially interesting because there has been some recent work by people at the University of Alaska at Fairbanks, they are Paleoclimate people. They found that in the higher latitudes it seems that the vegetation is precipitation limited. So even in a warmer climate, it doesn't necessarily mean that the trees will grow faster, they need the precipitation also.

"If the precipitation moves it does not necessarily mean that Alaska will become greener. So it is very complicated. It would probably be drier in the southern part of Alaska and wetter in the northern part." She stressed that, because the climate models aren't fine tuned, it isn't possible to predict precisely how the precipitation will change.

Our interview occurred in mid-January 2004 during a "cold" snap on the East Coast. "I even noticed this with people who are complaining on the East Coast about how cold it is. And I grew up in the east and I remember as a kid we had temperatures like that.

"People forget very quickly. And I even forget how cold it got, and I have to go back and look at the temperatures and the descriptions. I agree that Alaska has seen some dramatic changes if you look at the last 40 years. And there have been some big shifts in the circulation and the temperatures of the north Pacific. A lot of what is happening in Alaska is tied to what is happening over Siberia and the North Pacific where there have been changes in the circulation and changes in the ocean transport."

CHAPTER THREE

Traditional Knowledge Less Relevant in Changing Climate

In my week-long stay in Old Crow in the Yukon Territory in the Summer of 2004, there was much talk of climate change, and I did not have to ask about it. The Porcupine River had broken up far early, in May, and taken along with it several Gwich'in meat caches and a cabin, luckily with no one in it. The village government is putting in a permafrost research station to monitor the changes.

I was honored to attend the annual meeting of Old Crow, the General Assembly, which gives residents a chance to directly question tribal leadership. With caribou, moose, salmon, duck, geese, and ample food always available, along with coffee and tea, all focus for days was the issues at hand. Climate change was a major topic of the General Assembly, and there was no question that it was harming the Gwich'in way of life and the greater environment that they depend on.

Cindy Dixon, who works at the Coucil of First Nations spoke at the General Assembly. "Climate change is becoming a larger issue around the circumpolar Arctic," she said. "We're finding not just through science, but through our elders, our climate is changing. The migratory patterns are changing, the ice caps are melting. Inuit villages will have to move. Species are moving in that have not been there.

"The elders have for years been talking about the changes, and now scientists are documenting it. We also have an elder's panel. Elders want to be involved. They give us direction on how to do our work and where the findings should go. They want to know what animals are coming in. They're finding moose are moving elsewhere and deer are coming in. The Arctic is being affected first by climate change. They predict in 20 years the ice will be open (in the Arctic Ocean) and they will be shipping stuff back and forth. They're saying that's positive, but that could be the end of the Inuit cultures."

Elders reported that Musk-ox were found up in the mountains, which they said was caused by climate change. "We started to see a lot of animals and plants they've never seen," said Robert Bruce, Chief of Old Crow from 1991-1996. He said they drill the ice in the winter and where it was 6 feet thick every year a decade ago, now it was only 3 feet thick.

Speakers at a conference in Reykjavik, Iceland in November 2004 reported that Greenland hunters had to kill their own sled dogs that year because they were unable to feed them, as the late ice build-up meant the hunters were unable to hunt seals, polar bears and walrus.

Inuit report that drowning accidents are more common, as once peaceful waters have turned into torrential rivers because of melting glaciers. Hunters are having a harder time making protective igloos without as much or any snow when normally it was prevalent. Inuit fishermen complain of suffocating heat.

Sami reindeer herders have found that their herds, which normally dig through the snow with their hooves to get lichen, their main food source, are now unable to break through the thick layers of ice after rainstorms which are now common when it once snowed. Herders have reported an increase in calf mortality.

The weather is really unpredictable," said Gwich'in Sarah James. "There is extreme change. We don't have a healthy four seasons anymore. The cycle of the season is unpredictable, and that affects the animals that depend on those things. We have long, mild winters and all of a sudden it will change to real cold weather and that will kill animals. When there is too much extreme change, they can't adapt to that. Like fur animals, the fur buyers want furs from the middle of winter, that's when the fur is the shiniest and best. If the fur is not ready for cold weather, then the fur is not good.

"Sometimes in the winters it gets really warm, and that is not good for animals either. It makes the river flow, and it makes it hard for us to get wood and hunt." Wood is easier to harvest when the ground is frozen because transporting it is easier on a solid surface. "The ice breakup is unpredictable, too. Sometimes, it breaks up early, or stays too long. It used to be much more predictable. Now it is either later or early or sometimes on time."

Dan Ritzman worked for Greenpeace on climate issues in the Arctic from 1998 to 2000. "Greenpeace's focus was on the western Arctic because the Arctic is warming faster than any other area. One way to point out global warming is to get testimonies of the native peoples who have a closer connection to the land. We thought they could relay in their lifetime changes in the land that they have seen.

"For the people of coastal Alaska, subsistence is still an important part of their life. They talked about changes in the pack ice. It would come in later and go out earlier. There were more violent storms. There were earlier springs, changes in vegetation, more shrubbery and trees and occasional anecdotal evidence of new species in the ocean and land.

"We went to eight villages total. In each village we would have a general meeting—usually 20-30 people. Often we would focus on one or two people who were more articulate or had more to say. For us it was a pretty eye-opening experience. We believed climate change was happening. It was in the universal nature of what people were talking about. There were so many similar bits of anecdotal evidence it was hard to ignore them. The bumblebees are bigger. The ice is thinner, they would say. After you've gone to five or six places and the same similarities are said, it is hard to ignore."

Lakes like this one in the Yukon Flats region just south of the Arctic National Wildlife Refuge are drying out as the permafrost that once supported them melts, draining the water away. Photo by Chad Kister.

Susie Akootchook of Kaktovik reported that the warmer temperatures in the Beaufort Sea has made fishing more difficult because the fish no longer preserve like they used to when it was colder. "The weather in the ocean has tremendously warmed up. So much so that the fishermen have to check their nets out more frequently so the fish won't spoil due to the temperature of the water."

Writer Yereth Rosen reported on April 21, 2004 that "ANYONE who doubts the gravity of global warming should ask Alaska's Eskimo, Indian and Aleut elders about the dramatic changes to their land and the animals on which they depend." Rosen reported that native peoples of Alaska report that the salmon are increasingly susceptible to warm-water parasites and have lesions and odd behavior. Native peoples said salmon and moose meat have odd tastes and the marrows of moose bones are weirdly runny. Rosen reported in the Christian Science Monitor October 7, 2003 that temperatures in rivers in Alaska are 5 degrees warmer in the last 20 years, making them nearly lethal to salmon. "Warming may have dire consequences for salmon in the Yukon River, the major food source for indigenous people along the 2,300-mile waterway."

Southern Alaska is already reporting salmon kills because of increased temperatures. "The summers are getting hotter because of climate change," said Greenpeace volunteer Larry Edwards of Sitka. "So here in the South Tongass, we are having problems with overheating of salmon streams. Last summer, there were fish kills at Stanley Creek on Prince of Wales Island."

Three warm summers in a row have dried wells and forced the native village of Nanwalek to ship in bottled water and ration it, Rosen wrote.

Moses Lord, a Gwich'in from Fort Yukon said, "I remember growing up as a child, the snow used to stay around until the first of June, ice used to break up in mid June. Now it breaks up the first week of May. In the last few summers, it's cooler with lots of rain and warmer winters. We notice some lakes are draining out, while other lakes have more water."

Deborah Williams spoke about the plight of native peoples in Alaska because of climate change. "At our conference, Sterling Gologergen spoke. She is a Siberian Yupik who was born and raised on St. Lawrence Island. She talks very movingly about how global warming is undercutting Alaska native cultures, because Alaska native cultures rely so heavily on traditional knowledge. That traditional knowledge has been passed down from generation to generation. They rely so much on hunting and fishing and gathering.

"When it becomes harder to hunt because you don't have the ice to hunt on, or impossible to hunt, when your knowledge about how to hunt is no longer relevant because things have changed more dramatically, when people die more often hunting because they fall through the thin ice, or broken off ice, when the gathering of berries becomes more difficult because the conditions for berries in Alaska is much worse, it is so disruptive of cultures that Sterling believes that climate change will potentially lead to the destruction of the fabric of many Alaska native cultures and Siberian Yupik will be one of them."

Rosen reported that "Indigenous residents of the far north are finding it increasingly difficult to explain the natural world to younger generations." Larry Merculieff, an Aleut leader from the Pribilof Islands in the Bering Sea said, "As species go down, the levels of connection between older and younger go down along with that."

Charles Wohlforth, author of The Whale and the Supercomputer: On the Northern Front of Climate Change (2004) about perceptions of climate change in the Arctic said, "I think that with the warm weather that we have had in the last few years there has been a pretty broad awareness that something in the climate has changed. And I think that is pretty universally accepted."

Native Villages are being severely impacted by the receding pack ice, Wohlforth said. "The sea ice is much less reliable as a platform for hunting. This has several impacts. One is the increased danger because of ice breaking off and people floating out in the ocean on the ice." He said it is difficult to find ice strong enough to haul a whale up on the ice. The period of safe operations in the spring is shorter and more interrupted by dangerous incidents, which makes hunting less successful. In the fall the retreat of the sea ice has caused much larger waves to be present there along the Arctic coast, which means that hunting in boats is more dangerous because the waves are rougher. And it also dramatically increases the erosion on the shoreline.

"If you go closer to the southern edge of the ice pack around St. Lawrence Island, you have a situation where you have people that traditionally hunted on ice much of the year, but the ice just simply did not show up as much of the time as before. And this is true around Barrow too. There is less of the good time of hunting when there is plenty of light and when the ice is available."

During nearly three months of the Arctic winter, the sun never rises. It is in the fall and spring where native peoples had the overlap of sunlight and ice. But these are the times when the ice has decreased the most, cutting back on that critical time when hunting is the easiest.

Wohlforth said he chose the title of his book, "The Whale and the Supercomputer" because "you have the symbol of the two cultures. The topic that I had taken on, rather than trying to prove that one thing or another was going on, was more to explore how people are perceiving what was happening. I spent time in the field with scientists who were studying the snow and the tundra and the sea ice. I spent quite a bit of time with the subsistence whalers and talking to them about what kinds of changes they were seeing.

"It is about Eskimo whalers in Barrow and their traditional knowledge and science and perspectives on climate change and the cultural differences in how the two different cultures view the environment.

"I think it was very clear to everyone that something very dramatic is happening. It has already affected their way of life and how they pursue their subsistence. Having kind of a holistic or dynamic view of nature in some ways is a much better way to see and understand climate change and how it is happening. This contrasts with the sort of snapshot version or the computer climate-modeling version that the scientists produce. There is more certainty in actually living out nature and experiencing it and seeing how it changes through time as a native elder than as the scientists who plug a lot of data points into the computer to get an answer.

"There are warmer temperatures in the summer which make it more difficult to preserve meat that they have hunted out on the tundra. In my book I've tried not to oversimplify it or just pick out the evidence of climate change being a problem, but have also shown the complexity and all the different strands of what is going on.

"I think it is more of a matter of patterns. There is a different size of storms, and they tend to be larger. The value of traditional knowledge is not individualistic. It is based on a lot of people in the community who have worked together and developed a joint body of knowledge or a consensus on what is happening. A lot of the elders have said the weather has become less predictable."

The Arctic Research Consortium of the United States (ARCUS) published "The Earth is Faster Now: Indigenous Observations of Arctic Environmental Change" in 2002 about indigenous peoples in the Arctic and their observations of how the environment and climate has changed.

Wohlforth said, "When they say the Earth is faster now, they say that the Earth's systems move through quicker and are less predictable, and that fits in pretty well with the observations. What the elders are saying is the weather systems are moving through faster, they are less predictable and they are more violent. And after that observation was made by the elders there were some meteorologists who went out and studied the weather patterns and said 'by golly that is true.' The storms that are coming through are coming in on a more frequent rhythm than they normally did. That is something where the elders noticed something very subtle about the patterns of weather coming through and then the scientists went back and were able to confirm it in their own perspective.

"I don't think any of it is a big secret anymore. What I was concentrating on is more seeing it on a personal level, talking to individuals and what they were doing. I was more interested in writing about the environment as seen through peoples' eyes, and the cultural aspects of this whole issue."

Global warming has become a common term in the vocabulary of the people in Alaska, Wohlforth said. "Last winter (2002-2003) was the warmest winter that we had up here. There were phenomenon seen all over the state that were rarely ever seen before. Rivers never freezing, lack of snow cover, animals not hibernating that normally hibernate, insect populations exploding because there is not enough cold to kill them off during the winter, there are just huge numbers of unusual occurrences due to very warm winter conditions. We had several warm winters." Wohlforth said three winters in a row from 2001-2003 were all quite warm and there were a lot of impacts from it.

Wohlforth warned of the prediction of further warming in the far north. "The biological ranges at the furthest north will presumably disappear. You talk about the speculation of the pack ice disappearing, then presumably the habitat that relies on the pack ice disappears. That would also mean the Arctic tundra."

Chuck Hunt of Bethel spoke about the changes he has seen. "Let me speak about the weather change I've noticed since my childhood. When I was growing up, the weather of the four seasons was very definite. During winter, beginning in December until the mid-part of February, the temperatures were usually quite cold. Then the weather would begin warming as spring approached. In winter, the precipitation of snow was usually quite abundant. In some winters, we had so much snow, many of the houses were covered to the rooftops. When approaching a village in winter, all you could see were chimneys.

"In spring, the melt-off of snow and ice were normal. During the river ice break-up, on both the Yukon and Kuskokwim, it was normal to have floods due to the extra thickness of the ice and melt-off of snow.

"Summers were normal. In June and July we would have warm weather with clear skies, north winds and occasionally, thunder, lightning, and rain. But mostly, it was clear and warm. August would bring south winds ranging from 20-40 mph and much rain. In September when the weather cooled off, again the winds would be blowing from the north and bring clear skies. The rivers, sloughs, and lakes would freeze sometime in late October.

"It was in 1967 that I began noticing the weather changes when we had one week of rain which melted off most of the snow and ice we had in Bethel. This occurred during the month of January, which is considered to be the coldest month in the Y-K Delta. Since then our prominent wind direction in winter has been from the east, south, and west. Our snow precipitation in winter has also declined so badly that it is normal to have rain in December and January to the point where we would not have any snow on the ground, but bare tundra.

"One November our weather was so warm, the frozen Kuskokwim River ice almost melted off. Today, our summers have been quite different from the weather when I was growing up. Since 1967 or thereafter, our summers have been quite erratic with prominent winds from south, southeast, west, and southwest. These winds bring rain, high winds, fog, and drizzle. This 1999 summer has been quite wet with a few clear sunny days in between. June and July are usually nice sunny months with a few thunder and lightning days. But we have not seen any of those types of days for so long, we don't even know what thunder and lightning are anymore."

CHAPTER FOUR

Retreat of the Glaciers

With the increase in temperature, glaciers in Alaska are receding fast. A team of Alaskan researchers found that the rate of thinning has doubled in the past five years compared to the prior 40 years.

"Glaciers are formed by overflow of snow in the wintertime," said Gwich'in elder Sarah James. "Some of the glaciers get thawed out by the end of summer. Snow would be melting, there would normally still be snow or a glacier at the end of summer, but now it all melts."

The Columbia Glacier retreated nearly 13 kilometers between 1982 and 2000. In 1999 the retreat rate increased from 25 meters per day to 35 meters per day. The glacier now retreats at a rate of half a mile per year and has retreated eight miles in the last 16 years.

"The Columbia Glacier in southern Alaska began a catastrophic retreat in the mid 1980s," reported Michael Hambrey and Jurg Alean in "Glaciers," (1992). The retreat has caused a massive increase in icebergs. The prediction that these icebergs would be a hazard for boating proved true when the Exxon Valdez, carrying oil from the north slope of Alaska that had been pumped to Valdez through the Trans Alaskan Pipeline, tried to avoid ice from the Columbia glacier. While it avoided the ice, it ran aground (with the contributing factor that the captain was drunk), spilling 11 million gallons across more than a hundred miles of some of the most environmentally sensitive areas of the state. The contamination is still causing massive ecological impacts more than 15 years later.

"Ninety-nine percent of the temperate glaciers under a mile above sea level are receding, thinning or stagnant," said Glaciologist Bruce Molnia. "Most of those that are stagnant are

This photo is of the same area of what once was a glacier in Glacier National Park (top photo, 1937), that is now melted away (bottom photo, 1988)

insulated by rubble on top of them. Temperate glaciers are those that have both ice and water. They make up three percent of glacier ice and are the most sensitive to global warming." He said glaciers north of the Arctic Circle are melting as well. "The McCall glacier in the Brooks Mountain Range has been melting about a foot a year," Molnia said. "Most of the glaciers in Alaska are wasting away. Glaciers in Glacier Bay have retreated 60 miles since the 1800s. Scientists say the last decade of the 20th century is far warmer than the prior 4-5 decades.

"Polar ice, which is far below freezing, is a lot less sensitive. It may change from -60 to -50 degrees but it still will not melt. Polar ice is accumulating in Antarctica—it recently covered the U.S. base on the South Pole. But the edges of Antarctica and Greenland are melting."

"The thousands of glaciers in Alaska have seen dramatic losses," Weller said. "Some of the smaller glaciers are disappearing entirely, as is happening throughout the world, like Glacier National Park."

Glacier National Park had more than a hundred glaciers in 1900. By 1964, it was down to 67 glaciers. Now there are less than 37 remaining. Scientists predict there will be none left by 2030. Walking the hundreds of yards next to remnant ice packs that were once glaciers in the park, one can see the change vividly. Glacier Park rafting guide Denny Gignoux said, "you see the changes quite rapidly."

In Alaska, it is Glacier National Park on a far grander scale. "There are thousands of glaciers in Alaska and they are receding," Weller said, adding that melting from the Alaskan Glaciers adds the amount of water that would cover an area the size of Alaska five meters deep to the ocean. "It is a significant contribution to sea levels. The reduction in thickness and length in recent years have accelerated. They fly with a plane and use a laser altimeter to measure it. As they do that from year to year, they can measure the water loss."

Between 1850 and 1960, glaciers retreated 7.5 percent in

Alaska. Between 1960 and 2000, there was a 7 percent retreat, reported Ohio State University Geological Science Professor Dr. Lonnie Thompson in the *New York Times*, November 9, 2004. This is a rate of increase of nearly three times. The professor also documented large puddles of melting ice at 20,000 feet in the Himalayas, where for thousands of years all had been frozen. The melting is creating new lakes in the Himalayas as water accumulates behind dams of ice that could break, unleashing flash floods.

You can see the scale of melting in walking up to the massive glaciers. Their immensity, and the hundreds of yards of barren ground that had just been glacier the year before, are awakening people who frequent glaciated regions to the severity of global warming. In flying a bush plane over the Brooks Mountain Range of the Arctic National Wildlife Refuge in 2004, areas that had been glacier just 13 years prior, when I backpacked and rafted 700 miles through the refuge, were now all melted.

"I have lived up here for 23 years," Williams said. "Just going to Prince William Sound and seeing tidewater glaciers that you have experienced just a mere 10-15-20 years ago, you come around the bay and their retreat, their diminishment is breathtaking. It is like someone punched you in the stomach when you see these glaciers that once commanded this extraordinary presence in a bay or inlet but now are diminished and small. In a fraction of a lifetime to see that change again and again is incredible.

On Kilimanjaro in Kenya, an 11,700 year old ice cap that was 4.3 square miles in 1912 had retreated to .94 square miles in 2000 (*NYT*, 2004). Scientists predict that the ice cap will disappear in 15 years. "When you see the big picture accumulating from many sites, the evidence of drastic climate change becomes quite compelling, Dr. Thompson said (NYT 2004).

In addition to raising sea levels, glaciers can also increase the frequency of earthquakes in this, one of the most seismically active places on Earth. "Ebbing glaciers may make quakes likelier," read the *Washington Post* in October 2004. "Retreating glaciers in Southern Alaska may make earthquakes more likely there, according to a study by NASA and US Geological Survey Scientists." The paper reported that glaciers in Alaska had shrunk at least ten percent in the last hundred years. "As they melt, they lighten the load on the Earth's crust and allow the slowly drifting tectonic plates that make up the crust to move more freely. The collision of two plates under the Pacific Ocean off Alaska creates a buildup of pressure, which is relieved by earthquakes."

"This just makes it easier for earthquakes to occur," the *Post* quoted NASA Geophysicist Jeanne Sauber. "This is equivalent to years of tectonic strain accumulating." Sauber and Bruce Molnia co-authored a study revealing these findings in the July 2004 issue of the journal *Global Planetary Change*.

This is no laughing matter in what scientists say is the most seismically active place on Earth. An Alaskan state brochure on earthquakes reads, "It is no surprise to anyone who has lived in Alaska a few years that our state is one of the most seismically active regions of the world. Most of us have felt earthquakes at one time or another." Three of the world's six largest earthquakes have occurred in Alaska since the turn of the century. Earthquakes of a magnitude of 7 or greater have shaken some part of the state at least once a year, quakes of a mgnitude of 8 or greater have taken place once every 13 years on average.

In 1964, an earthquake of a magnitude 9.2 hit near Anchorage, killing a hundred people in Alaska and 16 people on the coasts of California and Oregon mostly from the massive wave, called a tsunami. The gaint wave triggered landslides and large scale destruction.

The phenomenon is not constrained to Alaska, but is worldwide. Greenland contains the largest mass of land-based ice outside of Antarctic, with eight percent of the world's ice. There, the ice sheet has thinned more than a meter per year on average since 1993 along parts of its southern and eastern edges.

University of Colorado at Boulder scientist Konrad Steffen found that 16 percent more Greenland ice melted in 2002 than in 1979, when satellite monitoring began.

The same warming weather around the far north is being felt in the far south as well. Scientists blame global warming for the disappearance of child-sized Adelie penguins from the northern tip of the Antarctic Peninsula, which juts out toward South America. The pack ice has become so scarce that the penguins can no longer use it as a resting platform for their winter fishing.

Antarctica, with 91 percent of Earth's ice and an average of 2.3 km. in thickness, is also melting. In the 1990s, three ice shelves along the edges of the Antarctic Peninsula have fully disintegrated. Two more ice shelves lost more than one seventh of their combined 21,000 square kilometers between late 1998 and March 2000, an area the size of Rhode Island.

Worldwatch Institute reports that as a whole, the world's glaciers are now shrinking faster than they are growing, and losses in 1997-1998 were "extreme," according to the World Glacier Monitoring Service. Scientists predict that up to a quarter of global mountain glacier mass could disappear by 2050, and up to one-half could be gone by 2100. In other parts of the world, Himalayan glaciers are expected to shrink by one-fifth, to 100,000 square kilometers in the next 35 years. In Nepal, melting ice prompted a glacier lake to burst in 1985, sending a 15-meter wall of water rushing 90 kilometers down the mountain, drowning people and destroying houses.

Ice-melt on land increases sea levels as it flows downstream into them. Over the past century, melting in ice caps and mountain glaciers has contributed on average about one-fifth of the estimated 4-10 inch rise in global sea levels. The rest is caused by the thermal expansion of the oceans as the Earth has warmed. But the share of ice melt in the rise of sea levels is increasing, and will continue to accelerate if the larger ice sheets crumble as expected.

The increase in water to sea levels threatens to flood low lying areas such as New Orleans, Florida, New York, Tokyo, Shanghai, Bangladesh, islands throughout the planet, much of the Netherlands and more.

Antarctica has 70 percent of the planet's fresh water. The collapse of the 360,000 square mile West Antarctic Ice Sheet (WAIS), an ice mass the size of Mexico, would raise sea levels by an estimated 6 meters—more than 18 feet (Nature, 1998). The melting of both of Antarctica's ice sheets would raise global sea levels by 70 meters. This is different than the melting of Arctic Ocean sea ice or the floating Antarctic ice shelves, which have no effect on sea levels because they already displace water.

NASA issued a report, "Vanishing Ice" on May 7, 2003 that began with the shocking find of Konrad Steffen, principal scientist and interim director at the Cooperative Institute for Research in Environmental Sciences (CIRES) at the University of Colorado, after returning to the Arctic where previously it had always been frozen. "Steffen arrived on the Greenland Ice Sheet for the 2002 summer fieldwork season and immediately observed that something significant was happening in the Arctic. Pools of water already spotted the ice surface, and melting was occurring where it never had before.

"That year the melt was so early and so intense—it really jumped out at me. I'd never seen the seasonal melt occur that high on the ice sheet before, and it had never started so early in the spring," said Steffen.

CHAPTER FIVE

The Melting Permafrost

The ground had collapsed, 15 feet into the earth. Two hundred miles above the Arctic Circle, just outside the Gwich'in native village of Arctic Village, the permafrost under the tundra had melted. I had been to the spot in 1991, and 1993. The collapse had just happened earlier in this, the summer of 2004.

In the Arctic, the land is supported by the permafrost—land which for millennia has been frozen year-round from a foot to 2,000 or more feet deep. The permafrost holds the lakes and streams in place. As it melts, lakes have drained and streams have eroded. In addition, all human structures in the two thirds of Alaska that has permafrost depend upon the frozen ground for support.

The permafrost is very important to the ecology of the Arctic, because much of it only receives about 8 inches of precipitation a year, about as much as a desert. The frozen ground holds that moisture up near the surface, and as the top foot thaws out every year, places like the coastal plain of the Arctic National Wildlife Refuge comprise some of the largest wetlands in the world, providing breeding habitat for millions of birds from around the world, hundreds of thousands of caribou, musk-ox, bear, wolf and much more.

But global warming is turning the permafrost into a soft, slurry-like material that can trigger subsidence (the collapse of surface lands) and damage to buildings, roads, trees, power-lines, pipelines and more. University of Alaska at Fairbanks studies indicate that a change in permafrost temperature from minus four degrees Centigrade to minus one degree Centigrade

Don't step back! This sinkhole occurred earlier in 2004, this photo taken in August 2004 near Arctic Village. As the permafrost melts, cavities of water cause sinkholes like this one, which was 20 feet deep. Let anyone who questions the reality of global warming fall into one of these. Photos by Chad Kister.

decreases the load capacity of permafrost by as much as 70 percent. All throughout the Arctic homes and buildings are being damaged by the warming, with cracks and fractures as the houses settle into the soft ground.

The melting has also caused severe erosion of rivers, streams, lakes and oceans throughout the Arctic. It has dried out many of the wetlands, destroying this critical habitat. The future promises to be far worse. While boating 300 miles down the Porcupine River from Old Crow in Canada to Fort Yukon in Alaska, I saw where the bank is eroding, and tundra collapsing down into the river, its former base of frozen permafrost melted and washed away.

The tundra holds together, and folds down where its base has gone like a carpet draped over the edge of a rooftop. I saw it too along Old John Lake, where I stayed for many nights, and backpacked along its shore. You could see the erosion in the water, where waves ate away at the thawing ground. Large cracks were around the lake, often more than a foot wide and several feet deep, awaiting the fate of the many avalanches of fallen earth that have already collapsed into the lake.

"In the last 10 years, we've seen a lot of changes," said Gwich'in Aaron Tritt in an interview in Arctic Village, the summer of 2004. "The permafrost is melting. The lakes are drying out. The tundra is collapsing. It used to be we went out hunting and it was noisy with all the wildlife and birds. Now it's quiet. We have told them what we can tell them. Even the Inuit know climate change is happppening. If we see that evidence (of climate change) in the last 10 years, what are we going to see in the next 15-20 years? Twenty years is not that long."

Compounding the situation, the melting permafrost itself releases greenhouse gases that further warm the planet. The frozen earth of the permafrost has locked carbon and methane, both greenhouse gases, for thousands of years. Svein Tgveitdal, director of the United Nations Environmental Program center in Norway reported, "there is now evidence that this is no longer the case, and the permafrost in some areas is starting to give back its carbon. This could accelerate the greenhouse effect."

An estimated 14 percent of the world's carbon is stored in Arctic lands. As the permafrost melts, and releases the gases, this causes further warming in a vicious cycle. As the permafrost melts, bacteria break down the organic material, releasing the ancient carbon.

Guntner Weller confirmed that the permafrost is melting. "As the climate begins to warm, the permafrost thaws, and with it comes pretty dramatic changes in the ecosystem. For example forests, especially if they have big ice masses, these melt, big holes develop and trees fall into it. We are seeing a change from boreal forests to wetlands and eventually over long intervals from wetlands to grasslands. We are beginning to see the beginning of that.

"Practically all the roads in the interior are built on permafrost. The increased warming and settling of the roads also has an economic impact. Most of the interior of Alaska is in this discontinuous permafrost. In the discontinuous zone, the permafrost is patchy, and only a few meters thick, and absent elsewhere. The discontinuous permafrost is very close to melting. Fairbanks has an average of 28 degrees F. It is very close to melting. Four degrees will melt it."

Pam Miller, with Arctic Connections said, "If there is permafrost under or around the lake that was frozen, holding in the water, it melts and they drain. When you are going from Arctic Village on the East Fork of the Chandalar River to the north, there is a place where a large piece of the bank has completely melted out. I've had people up there point that out to me. It looked like a pile of mud where there used to be a solid river bank."

Charles Wohlforth said, "Numerous people I talked to said that the active layer was deeper than it was formerly, that formerly you could dig down two feet in September and see ice. Now you can dig down two yards. People are talking about streams cutting through because of the melting of the permafrost." Previously, indigenous peoples dug into the permafrost to store meat through the summer in permanent iceboxes. But, Wohlforth said, "Natives report a change in their ice cellars and less ability to keep food frozen and things like that. Those are pretty common observations."

Traditionally, Inupiat peoples dig into the permafrost to store whale, caribou, seal, walrus, fish or other subsistence meat. But, global warming is melting the permafrost, requiring the Inupiat to consider providing refrigeration with electricity and freezers when previously such a "necessity" would have been laughed at in the far northern region.

"Today more and more, global warming is real in the Arctic," Sarah James said. "A lot of our lakes have been drying out around the villages and in the valley. It's because they were two bodies of water, the lake and the stream. But the permafrost melted and gave way and one of the lakes drained into the stream and it dried out. It displaced fish spawning and fish movement. The fish are dying out because of no water or less water."

James said the permafrost melting "changes our homes." Around Fairbanks, James said the concrete highways have a lot of patches in the concrete when it sinks in.

Dan Ritzman said the native peoples already knew about climate change before the scientists predicted it. "Western science was confirming evidence that these people knew. When asked, they knew it was getting harder and harder to feed their families on subsistence hunting because the weather was more severe, and there were fewer days in which they could hunt. Some had issues with lakes. The lakes would drain and they would catch fewer fish in the lakes."

"The coastal people are very focused on the ocean— that is their main means of subsistence," he said. The native peoples had gathered and hunted food for thousands of years, building a deep base of knowledge of how to survive. But now this subsistence is more difficult.

"It is very real up here," Miller said about climate change. "One time I flew between the Gwich'in village of Venetie and Arctic Village, and one of the women on the plane looked down and said 'Oh my God, is that lake gone?' It was one of the larger lakes (that dried out). It was empty of water. There are lakes that are drying up very fast in the interior and the Yukon Flats National Wildlife Refuge and throughout the southern part of the Arctic Refuge area, that general region. And it is very real in a different way than in the lower 48. If you travel to towns and say you are interested in global warming, every person you talk to just about has something to say about it."

Gwich'in Moses Lord of Fort Yukon said, "There's a big change in the land with the melting permafrost."

"We have collapsing highways, collapsing homes, you will see all of that when you come to Alaska," Williams said. "You have tipping light poles and so forth."

Charles Wohlforth said he gathered a lot of testimony about different changes in the distribution of snow, and the condition of the tundra. "The softer permafrost is causing streams to change course, and causing lakes to break through into one another."

"It is quite evident that the permafrost is being affected," Dr. Josefino Comiso said. "There are reports of electric pole lines toppling because the anchor was in the solid permafrost, but that is melting. And many parts of Alaska have been damaged because of the movement of the permafrost underneath."

CHAPTER SIX

Decreasing Pack Ice

From a mountain ridge in the summer of 2004, I gazed over miles of coastal plain of the Arctic National Wildlife Refuge and all the way to the blue of the Arctic Ocean. Thirteen years prior, at this same mid-August time period, the pack ice was along the shore, with just a narrow few hundred yards of open water. Now, there were tens of miles of open blue water before the specks of pack ice visible far, far away with the help of binoculars. There is no question that the pack ice is receding, and fast. Most do not understand the importance of the pack ice to the marine environment of the Arctic Ocean.

"The meeting of ice and open ocean habitats creates an unmatched richness of biodiversity of marine mammals," Greenpeace stated in its Answers from the Ice Edge report, June 1998. "Life concentrates at the ice edge, and its productivity each spring attracts an unmatched array of birds and mammals. Marine mammals from temperate climates venture north to feed on the seasonal abundance of Arctic waters. For other Arctic wildlife such as seal and walrus, ice provides transportation as well as a floating platform for resting, feeding and producing their young.

"Each winter Arctic pack ice advances across the Chukchi Sea and into one of the most productive marine ecosystems on earth — the Bering Sea. With the pack ice come animals that depend on it for life - bowhead and beluga whales, walrus, seal and polar bear. At this interface of ice and open water life flourishes and diversity of species is greatest. The richness of this marine life in turn attracts animals and people from the land. For thousands of years indigenous people of Alaska have relied on marine resources for food, clothing and cultural traditions.

"Climate change upsets the dynamics of marine and

coastal ecosystems and Native cultures that depend on them. The consequences of global warming are affecting the subsistence way of life of Alaska's Native peoples now."

"With satellite data seeing the entire globe, and seeing the extent of sea ice cover, we have seen a decrease in perennial sea ice cover of more than 20 percent," said Comiso. "Perennial ice is year-round ice. At ten percent loss of perennial ice per decade, you are looking at an ice- free Arctic Ocean by the end of this century.

"In 1998, there was a frozen ship in the Arctic, and they allowed it to move with the sea ice. It would move with the ice pack as the ice was affected by the ocean and the atmosphere. And at the end of the experiment, they get to the point where it is physically very far from Alaska, but they found out that the open water between Alaska and the ship was greater than they had ever seen. So we thought that 1998 was really a very dramatic year in terms of the amount of open water in the Arctic region. But in recent years, like 2002 and 2003, the open water was in fact larger."

The pack ice is at its largest in April. It retreats up to 1,700 kilometers, reaching its minimum area in September. The Arctic ice is twice the area at its maximum compared to its minimum. The advance and retreat takes the ice-associated animals to new feeding areas.

The annual drift of the pack ice is clockwise (anticyclonic) in the Beaufort Sea of the Canadian Basin, often referred to as the Beaufort Gyre or the Transpolar Drift Stream. The sea ice moves away form the Siberian coast, across the North Pole and exits the Fram Strait between Greenland and Svalbard. The freshwater current in the form of ice is twice as large as the combined discharge of the four largest rivers in North America.

The edge of the ice is not a sheer wall. It is a complex and ever-changing array of moving chunks of ice. It contains open water ponds called polynyas and long, linear cracks called leads.

The top satellite photo shows the polar ice cap in 1979, and the bottom photo shows the same area in 2001 at the same time of the year, with a massive reduction of the ice, particularly from Siberia, to the left of the photo, and Alaska on the bottom of the photo. The Bering Strait is on the bottom left corner of the photo. Photos by NASA.

Walrus and ringed, ribbon, bearded and spotted seals use ice as a platform to rest, mate and molt. Ringed seal are the northernmost seal, living not just in floes of the pack ice edge, but also in the thick ice of the far north. They mainly eat Arctic cod. Ringed seal are the principal food of the polar bear.

Ringed seal are the only seal to live on land-fast ice in winter, where they form an important source of food for indigenous peoples. In winter, tiny marine plants grow on the bottom of the ice. These plants form the base of the Arctic Ocean food chain. Crustaceans and other small animals feed on the algae. Arctic cod and other fish eat the crustaceans, with mouths that open forward and upward to feed off the floating ice.

As the pack ice retreats each spring, the luxuriant algae growth helps to seed the phytoplankton bloom (tiny floating plants) in the open Arctic Ocean waters. Fresh water from the melting ice floes forms a clear layer above the denser, darker sea water that allows ample sunshine to produce abundant plankton. The bloom is most intense as the ice breaks up. This plankton sinks after the ice retreats, feeding the bottom-dwelling or benthic communities such as clams, worms, amphipods and mollusks. Their abundance is so great that Grey whale migrate all the way from Baja California to feed along the retreating ice of the Bering Straight.

The Arctic sea ice, covering an area roughly the size of the United States, shrunk by an estimated 6 percent between 1978 and 1996, an area the size of Texas. Sea ice decreased an average of 37,000 square kilometers, an area larger than the states of Maryland and Delaware combined each year according to NASA Climatologist Claire Parkinson. NASA obtained this data from analysis of satellite pictures.

Even more alarming, between the 1960s and the mid 1990s, the average thickness in sea ice dropped from 3.1 meters to 1.8 meters, a decline of nearly 40 percent in less than 30 years according to a Worldwatch Institute news brief March 6, 2000.

"The direct evidence is from satellite data," Comiso said of the massive loss of ice in the Arctic. "We measure the surface temperature. Almost every kilometer of the Arctic is measured by the satellite, day in and day out. So we have this continuous record that then tells you which places are warming up and which places are cooling, just using trend analysis on this data.

"We have a different sensor that monitors the ice cover. This sensor is in the microwave region, where the wavelengths are low enough to be able to penetrate clouds without being affected too much. So this sensor is actually day and night continuous sensor to afford very detailed and consistent measurements of the surface. Over the years, we can compare what is going on with the ice cover and be able to analyze the data in a way that we can be sure that the sea ice is retreating or advancing. We have 25-30 years of satellite data, and we can see what is revealed from that data. We then try to extrapolate using that compared to surface data. Surface data is collected from meteorological stations all over the globe.

"We are consistent. In the Arctic there are not as many stations. It is very difficult to get measurements on areas covered with ice, because the areas covered by ice are not very easily accessed. Sometimes they freeze up ships in the ice pack and leave it there for a year with scientists on board a ship. And then the scientists can get out every now and then and take measurements." The scientists' boat is frozen into the ice "so they can take measurements of the meteorological data to help us understand what is going on in the Arctic region. This is one measurement from an area that is pretty big. So it is hard to say that one measurement can represent the Arctic."

Satellite data has enabled Comiso to measure the loss of pack ice. "The advantage of using satellite data is you get global coverage, and very specially detailed coverage over the whole Arctic region. What we know for sure is the behavior of the ice cover adjacent to Alaska. We have a very detailed data set from satellites over the last 25-30 years and it used to be that in the summer, the ice pack was pretty much accessible from the coastlines of Alaska, you know you could see it from the shore. But in recent times, the ice has retreated so much that it takes a major effort to get to the ice pack from the coastline of Alaska. In the Beaufort Sea in Alaska, the ice is retreating. The Beaufort Sea is the Sea adjacent to Alaska in the Arctic.

"What we have observed is over the last five years, starting in 1997, there was a little recovery in 2001, but in 2002 and 2003 the retreat was actually the worst. In fact you have the largest open water ever in the area adjacent to Alaska in the Arctic region. So in terms of the sea ice cover, a lot of things are really changing in the region." Satellite data reveals that that gap between the north shore of Alaska and the pack ice often well exceeds a hundred miles, when it used to never get more than 15 miles away, with major ramifications to wildlife that depend upon the ice edge to feed, rest and hunt.

Retired US Fish and Wildlife Service Arctic National Wildlife Refuge biologist Fran Mauer said, "there seems to be an increasing frequency of years when the ice was a long ways offshore. In recent years it has been quite far off shore, over a hundred miles away. The coastal erosion phenomenon has increased from the open water."

Alaskan Senator Ted Stevens reported a decrease in Alaskan ice by eight inches in 2003 compared to 2002. Submarine sonar measurements confirmed that average Arctic ice thickness in late summer since the 1950s have shown a decline to 5.9 feet in 2000 from 10.2 feet, a 42 percent decrease. The normally year-round ice is shrinking twice as fast as the overall winter perimeter, which has further alarmed scientists, and has several predicting that the Arctic Ocean will be ice-free in 50 years.

The loss of the pack ice and the corresponding algae threatens fish, seal, whale and polar bear. The ice edge creates the primary food source of phytoplankton for the Arctic ecosystem. It also is critical habitat for resting, feeding and hunting for most of the marine mammals as well as the Inuit native peoples who hunt them for food and clothing.

Like permafrost melting, the melting pack ice causes further warming of the globe. Arctic ice is white, and reflects 80-90 percent of the sun's heat back into space. Open water is much darker, and absorbs 80-90 percent of the sun's energy. The more that the ice sheet retreats, the warmer the ocean becomes. The increase in warming is called a feedback loop and the potential for increased warming alarms scientists.

Harley Sorenson, in an article, "A Warning From The North Pole," in the San Francisco Examiner on August 22, 2000 wrote, "The thick ice that covers the Arctic Ocean at the North Pole has melted, leaving a mile-wide stretch of water at the top of the world, The New York Times reported Saturday." The Harvard scientist who reported the open water at the North Pole made the same trip six years ago and that time saw ice six to nine feet deep.

"The extent of ice in the part of the Arctic covered by these new charts has decreased by about 33 percent over the past 135 years," says Lynn Rosentrater, a climate change scientist at World Wildlife Fund. "We believe this is due to global warming caused by burning fossil fuels. With the new data available in the sea ice charts, we can more easily study climate variability over a longer period of time and confirm our hypothesis."

"Associated with the temperature increases, we have seen a lot of impacts on snow and ice," Guntner Weller said. "The snow and ice are also good indicators of change. We have seen a fairly dramatic decrease in sea ice in the west and in the Arctic Ocean. In recent years the rate of loss has increased. Last year was the lowest (amount of ice) we have ever seen.

"These are some of the physical impacts occurring in Alaska. Associated with that is a lot of societal impacts. The native villages rely very heavily on subsistence. Marine mammals: seal, walrus and whales are affected by the change in the sea ice. Since many of these sea mammals rely on the sea ice to lie out, and for procreation, the decrease in ice is having a negative affect on them. Walrus must lie in shallow water to dive.

The disappearance of sea ice can be equated to a loss or displacement of the sea mammal habitat.

"The thickness is measured from sonar records from nuclear submarines. Declassified Navy data looks at thickness reduction. From the early 50s there are a lot of U.S. and some British nuclear submarine data. They have found a reduction in thickness of 40%, which is enormous. The average thickness was 9-12 feet. When they did it recently, we are down to 7 or 8 feet, which is really quite an enormous decrease.

"In the marginal fields, on average it was six feet thick; the reduction is almost the same, so we are down to three-four feet. There is a very enormous change in the observed thickness that has been documented. It could in part be displacements by storms, shifts in ice from one area to another, but it seems very likely that most of it is due to melting of the ice rather than shifting from one corner to the next."

Weller said the location and thickness of the ice in any detail is a classified military secret, which has hindered the study of climate change in the Arctic. "The navy did not want to release the precise locations of the data. There is a lot more submarine data out there that has not been declassified, and there is a lot of Russian data that has not been declassified.

"On the underside of the ice there is a fairly thick phytoplankton bloom in spring. The underside is a pretty thick mat of phytoplankton, and the zooplankton depends on that. You remove the ice, you remove the phytoplankton mat, and that certainly could affect the whole food chain."

A report by Cynthia Tynan and Douglas DeMaster for the Arctic Institute of North America published in December 1997 found that ice-associated seals rely on the pack ice for resting, pupping and molting, and "may be especially vulnerable" to the receding ice. The report also warned that the receding ice could affect the density and distribution of ice-associated prey of marine mammals such as arctic cod and sympagic (with ice) amphipods. Arctic cod have disappeared from the west coast of

Greenland around the island of Disko where temperatures have risen about four degrees Celsius over the past 15-20 years.

In his interviews with indigenous peoples, Dan Ritzman said, "It was so much about the pack ice because that is so critical to their subsistence. From the indigenous peoples' point of view, it was more about their ability to get out and hunt. The ice is a platform for them to go out and hunt. If the ice is not there, they could not go out to hunt. That is what was limiting their hunting. In Wainwright and Barrow, because the pack ice was receding further, the whales were farther north, so it was more dangerous to go out to get them."

CHAPTER SEVEN

Walrus

Walrus are very social animals, often clinging to each other with their flippers. They were once hunted to near extinction, but have since largely recovered. Walrus use their tusks to walk on the ice. In the water, walrus use whiskers to feel for clams, their main diet. They need thousands of clams a day, leaving large areas strewn with shells that are stripped of their meat.

"The science says the loss of pack ice will harm the numbers of walrus," Dan Ritzman said. "Walrus rest on the pack ice and feed on the bottom. The Arctic Ocean is fairly shallow, but the farther north you go, it drops off deeper. With the receding pack ice, it is getting too deep for the walrus to be able to rest on the pack ice and dive to the bottom to feed."

Spring brings patches of thin and thick ice. Inuit say that walrus bulls are fat, but smart. Walrus will break through the ice, then anchor themselves with their tusks on the ice while they rest and breathe. Inuit will wait a whole day until the ice gets right to get to the walrus. Inuit are allowed to hunt three walrus per year. They shoot the walrus then use a harpoon to pull the animal near. They secure more harpoons. Several other hunters abandon their hunts and come to the gunshot to help haul the walrus up, then carve up the carcass. They often have to rush to finish before the setting sun. There will be fresh meat for all. Nothing is wasted. Inuit will finish by washing their boots in the ocean, teetering over the ice edge, with one hand using a long knife for the stability lost with the foot being washed in the ocean.

In spring, walrus haul up on pancake ice to bathe in the sun. Sea birds arrive. Arctic cod darken the depths. Ringed seal get plump. Seal make a high-pitched, eerie communication. Polar bear troll the water, looking for young seal and walrus.

Walrus. Photo courtesy of the National Oceanic and Atmospheric Administration.

Walrus mothers will stay with calves for two years or more.

Walrus will frequently hug their babies with their flippers. Other walrus will sometimes help a mother and calf. With melting ice, often they get too crowded on the shrinking patches of ice. Walrus will display their tusks menacingly. When two evenly matched male walrus won't budge, a fight will ensue. They charge at each other with tusks. Shrinking ice forces walrus to fight more for the dwindling ice.

Walrus have air patches in their cheeks that help them float. They can sleep afloat with their cheeks inflated. Fifteen million years ago, walrus predecessors went into the sea. Now, they gather on rocky islands in the spring to rear their young in the protection of a herd.

Walrus have a hard time staying cool when hauled out on the rocks. As they get hot, they also get sleepy. When they molt in the spring, they itch. They sleep and snore. When a whole herd is asleep, polar bear attack. A polar bear will go through a precarious rocky descent on the opposite side of the island then swim around to hunt the walrus from the sea. By surprising the slumbering walrus from the sea, the more vulnerable females and calves will be the closest, as the males are on the side of the herd farthest from the ocean. Walrus go to thin ice, where polar bear tire because they cannot rest from treading water.

Alan Springer, a University of Alaska at Fairbanks wildlife specialist, said that the quarter million walruses in Alaska appear to have suffered weight loss and stress from the decrease of pack ice that they need for resting and raising their pups.

One year, walrus climbed high on a hill, then tried to take a shortcut to the sea. They followed a herd that went down a hill too steep for their ability. They tumbled down and over a bluff, one by one, crashing into a mound of dying bodies. Sixty walrus died that year. Similarly, U.S. foreign policy of opposition to the Kyoto Protocol is pushing our global environment over the edge of no return. It is up to us to change to a saner policy of survival.

CHAPTER EIGHT

The Decline of Black Guillemots

Black Guillemots also live in the Arctic islands, and depend upon the edge of the sea ice. They have orange feet and in the summer, they are all black except for a white patch on the top of their wings and a white underside of their wings. In the winter they turn mostly white. Guillemot is the common name for three species of birds in the auk family, two of which live in North America. They breed on coasts and islands, like other auk species, nesting in dense colonies unlike other members of the auk family. They hide in crevices of the cliffs overlooking the Arctic Ocean, raising their young. It is near impenetrable for predators. Guillemot chicks will jump off the cliff and glide to the ocean. Those who stay on land are eaten by glaucous gulls and Arctic fox.

Mother guillemots will call to their young, begging them to jump to the sea. Adults will escort them down. Gulls will catch those that are not escorted. Those that do not jump to the sea sometimes get lost, wandering around helplessly on the cliff tops. They are easy prey for Arctic fox and gulls. But, scientist George Devoky found that the guillemots are in serious decline, attributable to global warming.

"Darcy Frey did a New York Times Magazine cover story on George Divoky's work and is now doing it into a book," Deborah Williams said. The article is called "Watching the World Melt Away." "George was another scientist just minding his own business doing research on birds, black guillemots in a small island north of Barrow. He had been walking these islands and discovered an island with some guillemots on it." Divoky had not been aware that they were that far north. Divoky has

researched at Cooper Island, 530 kilometers north of the Arctic
Circle for 29 years. "There was a lot of military debris on the
island, you know boxes and crates and so forth," Williams continued. "He began turning them over to make nesting sites,
because he realized that nesting sites were the limiting factor"
for the guillemot population.

"He found that if he made nesting sites more birds would
come and propagate. He was doing this experiment about
guillemots and nesting sites and it was quite fascinating. The
populations grew and grew as the nesting sites increased. What
he found was then the nesting sites started declining. The
decline was corresponding to how far the birds had to fly to get
to the ice edge, because they were feeding on the highly productive ice edges. That is where the parents would go out to get
food for their young.

"The ice edge was retreating year after year after year, and
the birds had to expend more energy to fly out to the ice edge
to get the little fish that they feed on, there was greater and
greater nest failure." In 2003, when the ice edge was at its furthest, Divoky reported a 90 percent nest failure. "What you can
find with global warming is in so many instances it makes feeding so much more difficult. You have increased mortality associated with that. That is a profound impact," Williams said.

Divoky found that the guillemot chicks were starving, as
their parents could not make it out to the ice edge and back
with food, the distance being so great. The scientist also reported behavior he had never seen before, such as males choosing
two females instead of one because starvation meant there were
not enough mates, and chicks walking away from their nests in
search of food and foster parents.

Divoky discovered that the snow was melting five days
earlier each decade since his study began. The guillemots were
laying their eggs five days earlier as well, coinciding with the
earlier melting. Frey quoted Divoky as saying, "birds (are) non-
political. They have no choice but to react." That is what we,

humans, as the unquestionable cause of this increased warming, need to do as well. We must work with all of our power to stop our emissions of greenhouse gases, the cause of this problem. Divoky said, "You get these people who say 'Do you really think it's happening?' and I'm like, 'What is it you don't understand?'"

Divoky was quoted on National Public Radio on February 16, 2004 as saying, "I just hope you care about what the guillemots are telling us. And I think that this sort of rapid rate of change—that in three decades, and even within the length of one study, to see this much change indicates that things are happening globally that humans have to take note of."

CHAPTER NINE

The Fate of the Polar Bear

Scientists predict the polar bear will likely be extinct in the wild by 2100 with current global warming trends. The polar bear evolved from the grizzly bear, turning all white to blend in with the ice of the Arctic Ocean. But that ice is melting, and scientists question whether the bear will survive.

"There are some projections that predict that there will be an ice-free ocean by mid-century or shortly thereafter, which would spell a disaster for polar bears," Gunther Weller said. "We had a situation last fall, when the freeze-up occurred late and the polar bears could not get out on the ice. There was an accumulation of polar bears at Barrow that has never been seen before. They became a nuisance."

Polar bears have suffered a 15 percent decrease in their number of offspring and a similar decline in weight over the past 25 years, according to the Arctic Climate Impact Assessment Council, an international commission of eight countries, including the US and six indigenous groups in a November, 2004 report. The report was written by a team of 300 scientists. With predictions of an ice-free ocean later this century, the Arctic report questions whether the polar bear will survive in the wild.

The World Wildlife Fund (WWF) found that in the southern range of polar bears, for example the Hudson and James Bays of Canada, sea ice is now melting earlier in the spring and forming later in the autumn. The time bears have on the ice, storing up energy for the summer and autumn when there is little available food, is becoming shorter. As the periods without food become longer, the overall body condition of the polar bears declines. This is particularly serious for bears that are pregnant or have cubs, and for the cubs themselves. In Hudson Bay, scientists have found the main cause of death for cubs to be either lack of food or lack of fat on nursing mothers.

For every week earlier the ice breaks up in Hudson Bay, bears come ashore roughly 10 kg (22 lbs) lighter and in poorer condition according to WWF. Rising temperatures in the Arctic, therefore, mean less sea ice, leading to less healthy bears. Reduced body condition can lead to lower reproduction rates, which in the long run could lead to local extinction. According to the WWF, climate models predict that the Arctic Ocean could be ice-free by 2080.

"Polar bears are the largest land predators in the world," Deborah Williams said. "They are extraordinary animals that have evolved and adapted magnificently to their challenging environment. And polar bears need ice. When you deprive polar bears of ice and they get stranded on land, several things happen. One, they don't have their food source: seals and so forth. Two, they are more likely to be killed, 'in defense of life and property.' So you have a lot more human-caused mortality of polar bears. And three, polar bears become more engaged in fighting amongst themselves."

In addition to a loss of habitat, the massive reduction in ice extent also reduces the overall food levels in the Arctic Ocean, scientists warn. Dr. Vera Alexander of the Fisheries and Ocean Science Department at the University of Alaska, has been observing dramatic changes in temperature and ice-edge extent for the past 20 years. An expert on ice-edge ecology, Alexander stated that the continued decline of the sea ice will affect the production of algae, which live beneath the ice, and form the very base of the arctic food chain. "Without the ice algae," Alexander noted, "there would be no possibility of a food chain as we know it." The resulting impacts would ripple up the food web affecting fish, seals, whales and polar bears.

Glacier National Park rafting guide Denny Gignoux said,

"I spent time in Churchill and Manitoba, and you see the changes quite rapidly. The polar bears need to go out on the pack ice and feed. Without that, they don't feed. They need it to be strong enough to head out on Hudson Bay. They can't go out and get seals, so they just hang out and go hungry. It is very well documented with the World Wildlife Fund. Just a couple of degrees would make a difference in pack ice so the polar bears can't feed. We'd see anywhere from 3 to 30 every day."

Dr. Comiso said that "sea ice is a habitat for polar bear and many other animals. The sea ice is not a permanent habitat. It is a floating entity, on top of the ocean. You would think that polar bear have stable habitat. But as this ice retreats, then this platform that the polar bear uses to catch fish for example, or find food will not be available anymore."

NASA satellite photos of the ice in 1979 compared to the ice in 2003 shows a remarkable difference. The ice is hundreds of miles off the coast of Siberia whereas it once rarely went more than a few miles. This extension of ice from the coast has moved east from Siberia, opening water for great waves and increasing the distance to food for marine animals and native peoples who used to have food near the Northwestern Alaskan shoreline.

Retired U.S. Fish and Wildlife Service Arctic National Wildlife Refuge biologist Fran Mauer said, "There seems to be an increasing frequency of years when the ice was a long ways offshore. In recent years it has been quite far off shore, over a hundred miles away. The coastal erosion phenomenon has increased from the open water."

This ice retreat reduces food for polar bear near shore. "The thinning and the moving of the ice pack so far offshore changes the spatial relationship of food webs and animals that rely on the pack ice," Mauer said. "The spatial relationship changes. Seals and some of the other marine mammals that associate themselves with the ice are no longer close to shore at certain times of the year.

"There seems to be an increasing number of polar bears found along Alaska's coastline in late summer and fall in the last 5-6 years. They seem to be getting off the ice and staying onshore. It looks like a pattern somewhat similar to the Hudson Bay situation, with bears onshore when the ice is so far off shore. The Hudson Bay situation is different in that they spend the whole summer and fall onshore. When the bay freezes in early winter they go back out on the ice. But in this case they seem to show up in late summer and early fall on the Arctic coastline and tend to clump around places where Eskimo hunters have brought in whales. They are clumping around those whale carcasses.

"The numbers of bears (stranded on shore) have been increasing compared to what people used to see. During summertime it was an unusual event to see a polar bear along the shoreline. Not totally unheard of, but unusual. Now in late summer in the last few years, the numbers of bears and observations of bears has dramatically increased." Mauer said the unusual clumping of bears have been found around Barrow and Kaktovik where the whales are brought in in late summer.

Once considered a nuisance, people would set traps with bait and a gun that fired when the bear stuck its head inside. Now, we attack the bears with pollution, as well as guns. Pollutants travel from up to a thousand miles away. They bio-accumulate in the top predators, like seal who eat Arctic cod. Polar bear-eating seal get the most toxins. Polar bears have high concentrations of PCBs in the mother's milk. Those with the highest levels also have the highest rate of cub mortality.

Polar bear dens have a narrow opening. When they set out from the den to hunt, they often never return. Polar bear use snow dens, and the early spring melts could expose cubs too early in their development to the harsh Arctic weather. Mother bears must wait until their cubs are strong enough and quick enough to keep up before she can venture out to hunt and replenish her dwindling fat. Bears follow the retreating pack ice, hunting seal. Those bears that get stranded, get hungry. With the pack ice retreating earlier and so much farther, this is occurring far more often, to the detriment of the bears. On land, polar bear will eat eggs and young ducks. Arctic terns, which fly 22,000 miles every year from the Arctic to the Antartctic, will dive-bomb polar bear and hit them on the nose with the bird's feet to protect their eggs, often successfully saving them.

Smaller polar bear will wait until larger bears with successful kills get full, and tired. They will then stalk up and feed on the carcass, always ready to run from an awakening bear. But the over-stuffed successful hunter is often slow to awake and even slower to stir beyond the slight gruff necessary to send the young bear scampering away. Bears must wait for the return of the pack ice for seal.

Polar bears swim with their front paws and steer with their rear. They will roll in the snow to dry off or to clean themselves of blood after eating. Male and female will play with each other. Polar bear wag their heads back and forth to show they're angry.

Williams said that as a result of climate change, the animals are not getting enough food, and suffer as a result. "We are seeing some more profound impacts on polar bear around Canada and Hudson Bay, which is the southerly part of the bear's range. I think we are ultimately going to find tremendous impacts on polar bears. I am personally desperately worried about the plight of the polar bear."

CHAPTER TEN

Pentagon Calls Climate Change More Serious Threat Than Terrorism

A hundred thousand dollar Pentagon report that the Bush administration attempted to suppress calls climate change a more serious threat than terrorism, according to the *Observer Guardian*. The report details how climate change could result in a global catastrophe costing millions of lives in wars and "natural" disasters.

The Pentagon documented reports that abrupt climate change, which is like the tipping of a canoe that may start relatively calmly, then plunge over in violent upheaval, could bring the planet to the edge of anarchy as countries develop nuclear weapons to defend against dwindling food, water and fossil fuel energy supplies (the cause of the climate change problem to begin with).

The threat of climate change to global stability vastly eclipses that of terrorism, the report reads. The Pentagon report states, "Disruption and conflict will be endemic features of life. Once again, warfare would define human life." The British Observer-Guardian reported, "The findings will prove humiliating to the Bush administration, which has repeatedly denied that climate change even exists. Experts said that they also will make unsettling reading for a President who has insisted national defense is a priority."

The report was commissioned by Defense Advisor Andrew Marshall, a leading Pentagon official for the past 30 years, who is called the "yoda" of the Pentagon by insiders. It reads, climate change "should be elevated beyond a scientific debate to a US national security concern."

The Pentagon report found that, "Rather than decades or even centuries of gradual warming, recent evidence suggests the possibility that a more dire climate scenario may actually be unfolding."

Fortune Magazine said, "The threat that has riveted their attention is this: Global warming, rather than causing gradual, centuries-spanning change, may be pushing the climate to a tipping point. Growing evidence suggests the ocean-atmosphere system that controls the world's climate can lurch from one state to another in less than a decade—like a canoe that's gradually tilted until suddenly it flips over. Scientists don't know how close the system is to a critical threshold. But abrupt climate change may well occur in the not-too-distant future. If it does, the need to rapidly adapt may overwhelm many societies—thereby upsetting the geopolitical balance of power."

The report also warns that climate change will make a future with the borders of the U.S. and Australia being patrolled by armies firing into waves of starving boat people desperate to find a new home. Fishing boats will be armed with cannons to drive off competitors and demands for access to water and farmland are backed with nuclear weapons. Greenpeace called the Pentagons warnings as a "coming climate Armageddon." Sir David King, Chief Scientist in British Prime Minister Tony Blair's government, also said that global warming is a greater threat than terrorism.

The Observer reported key findings of the Pentagon Report as the following:

Future wars will be fought over survival rather than religion, ideology or national honor.

Violent storms smash the coastal barriers of Holland by 2007, rendering large parts of the country uninhabitable. The delta island levees in the Sacramento River area will be breached in California, disrupting the aqueduct system transporting water from north to south.

Similarly, an independent panel appointed by the World Bank recommended that the institution phase out investments in fossil fuels within eight years and aggressively invest in renewable energies for the needed transition into fuels that do not cause global warming. The panel wrote, "The WBG (World Bank Group) should aggressively increase investments in renewable energies by about 20 percent annually. WBG lending should concentrate on promoting the transition to renewable energy." Unfortunately, World Bank leaders do not plan to follow their consultants' advice.

Meanwhile "President" George Bush said, "The jury is still out." Greenpeace released a statement February 22, 2004 stating, "Actually, Mr. Bush, the jury's been in for some time, and now even a report commissioned by your own Pentagon is saying you're wrong. Perhaps it's time you focused on the real terrorist threat to our planet: the oil companies like Exxon which continue to fund your re-election, and whose interests you continue to defend at the expense of our future.

"While you're pursuing policies that accelerate the production of greenhouse gases and continuing to deny the existence of a threat, the World Bank is being told it has to stop subsidizing Armageddon, and the Pentagon is war-gaming ways to survive a catastrophe it's calling plausible.

"If you were willing to launch a pre-emptive war on enemies you believe may someday think about attacking the US, wouldn't it seem prudent to take pre-emptive action against climate change?"

The Pentagon warns of a climate spiraling out of control with the feedback loops of greater warmth and ecological catastrophe. The following is the prediction by Pentagon leaders:

As temperatures rise throughout the 20th century and into the early 2000s potent positive feedback loops kick-in, accelerating the warming from .2 degrees Fahrenheit, to .4 and eventually .5 degrees Fahrenheit per

year in some locations. As the surface warms, the hydro-
logic cycle (evaporation, precipitation, and runoff) accelerates, causing temperatures to rise even higher. Water
vapor, the most powerful natural greenhouse gas, traps
additional heat and brings average surface air temperatures
up. As evaporation increases, higher surface air temperatures cause drying in forests and grasslands, where animals
graze and farmers grow grain. As trees die and burn, forests
absorb less carbon dioxide, again leading to higher surface
air temperatures as well as fierce and uncontrollable forest
fires. Further, warmer temperatures melt snow cover in
mountains, open fields, high-latitude tundra areas, and
permafrost throughout forests in cold-weather areas. With
the ground absorbing more and reflecting less of the sun's
rays, temperatures increase even higher.

By 2005 the climatic impact of the shift is felt more
intensely in certain regions around the world. More severe
storms and typhoons bring about higher storm surges and
floods in low-lying islands such as Tarawa and Tuvalu
(near New Zealand). In 2007, a particularly severe storm
causes the ocean to break through levees in the
Netherlands making a few key coastal cities such as The
Hague unlivable. Failures of the delta island levees in the
Sacramento River region in the Central Valley of
California creates an inland sea and disrupts the aqueduct
system transporting water from northern to southern
California because salt water can no longer be kept out of
the area during the dry season. Melting along the
Himalayan glaciers accelerates, causing some Tibetan people to relocate. Floating ice in the northern polar seas,
which had already lost 40% of its mass from 1970 to 2003,
is mostly gone during summer by 2010. As glacial ice
melts, sea levels rise and as wintertime sea ice extent
decreases, ocean waves increase in intensity, damaging
coastal cities. Additionally millions of people are put at
risk of flooding around the globe (roughly 4 times 2003
levels), and fisheries are disrupted as water temperature
changes cause fish to migrate to new locations and habi-

tats, increasing tensions over fishing rights

Fortune Magazine reported in 2004,

> Though triggered by warming, such change would probably cause cooling in the Northern Hemisphere (around the Atlantic), leading to longer, harsher winters in much of the U.S. and Europe. Worse, it would cause massive droughts, turning farmland to dust bowls and forests to ashes. Picture last fall's California wildfires as a regular thing. Or imagine similar disasters destabilizing nuclear powers such as Pakistan or Russia—it's easy to see why the Pentagon has become interested in abrupt climate change.

Boating down the Porcupine River from Canada into Alaska in 2004. Photo by Chad Kister.

CHAPTER ELEVEN

Sea Coasts Crumble Into Sea

Coastal erosion along the north and west coasts of Alaska has even the notoriously anti-environmental Alaskan Senator Ted Stevens admitting that climate change is real and causing massive damage to the state. Two villages, Shishmaref and Kivalina have decided to move at a cost of more than a hundred million dollars each. The General Accounting Office (GAO) found that flooding or erosion regularly affects 86 percent of the state's 213 predominantly Native villages. The GAO predicted in a 91-page report in December, 2003 that four villages, including the two mentioned above, are in imminent danger. Newtok, where the Ninglick River erodes 90 feet of bank a year will have to move in five years according to the report, and Koyukuk must move soon as well.

Five other villages are threatened by the erosion, Kaktovik (293 residents), Point Hope (population 757), Unalakleet (with 747 people) and the regional hubs of Barrow (population 4,581) and Bethel (population 5,471) have airport runways, roads and other facilities threatened by erosion.

Stevens predicted that Barrow will also have to relocate. With 4,800 residents, its cost would be exponentially larger than the mammoth efforts necessary to move Shishmaref and Kivalina. "We face the problem of moving native villages that have been located along the Arctic and West coast of Alaska for centuries because they are slowly but surely being inundated by seawater," Stevens told five top climate scientists testifying before the Senate Commerce Committee.

"In the coastal zone, the impacts of climate change are

more severe," said Guntner Weller. "In two villages, Kivalina
and Shishmaref, the coastal erosion is getting so severe they are
forced to move the village at a cost of a million dollars per person. The cause of this coastal erosion is three-fold. As the permafrost thaws, the coast collapses. Second, with the glaciers
melting, sea levels rise, causing coastal erosion to increase.
Third, more open water allows storm surges to develop stronger
and more severely. The larger fetch area (open water) has caused
many more frequent storm surges and severe storm surges."

"On erosion, we are fairly certain that it has been accelerated much by climate change" Weller said. "It is true that there
has been erosion in the past, but the rate of it has been greatly
increasing. Now there is a legal argument, as to who pays for it.
Is it really the oil industry or the over-consumption of fossil
fuels? I think there is good evidence that this impact is caused by
global climate change. It is true that the Arctic coast is pretty
dynamic. It has occurred before, but never at this magnitude."

"Global warming's impact on infrastructure has been well
documented," Deborah Williams said. "It is most profound in
terms of impacts on coastal communities. We now have several
coastal communities that are being washed into the ocean and
must be moved. Sishmaref is the most impressive, or depressing
example of that. What you have with these coastal communities is generally three impacts going on at the same time. One is
the permafrost on which they sit is melting. Two is that sea levels have increased. And three is that in the past when you had
ice covering the Bering Sea or the Chukchi Sea for so much of
the year, particularly the spring and fall, when the winds came,
it didn't create waves. But when you don't have ice — and they
have fewer days of ice on the Bering Sea and Chuckchi sea —
the winds create wave action and the waves erode the banks of
the village.

"It is a very dramatic loss to these communities, and very
expensive. It will cost a hundred million dollars at minimum to
move these coastal communities. This not only has economic

costs, it has profound social costs. This is where indigenous people have lived for thousands and thousands of years, so they are losing their homelands."

"The waves need room to build up," Charles Wohlforth said. "In former times, there were less times when there was a gap between the shore and the ice. In the fall, which is a stormy time of year, if the ice is near shore, regardless of the strength of the wind, the waves would not get that large. Now for the last two years we have record low amounts of ice extent. There is more open water than ever before. The result of that is you get these big sea waves that come crashing into the shore during storms or just during normal conditions because there is hundreds of miles of open water out there. That has very clearly caused accelerated erosion, but again it is difficult to tell exactly how much because the shore of the Arctic is not that very well mapped. It is hard to tell what was there previously."

"There is much discussion about how much erosion has been caused," Wohlforth said. It is difficult because the erosion issue is always confounded by other conditions. The Corps of Engineers dredged a lot of gravel near Point Barrow. So some people blame the Corps of Engineers for the erosion from the dredging 30 years ago.

"There is the village of Shishmaref which is basically washing away. But then there are those that say that may have washed away anyway because it is a barrier island. So a lot of these things have counter arguments. It is hard to summarize what everyone up there feels, I did not take a public opinion poll, but I think there is a pretty good consensus that erosion has accelerated recently. There is also a cultural impact which is that prior to the missionaries and the villages coming into their modern form, there was always erosion, and there has always been areas that have washed away and people just moved. You know there was this flexibility in dealing with that. Now they have villages with roads and electric systems and school buildings and it is a lot harder to move. Or it is not harder to move, but you have a large dollar investment, so they are much more inclined to be rigid and so then erosion matters a lot more."

"In Shishmaref and the Bering and Chukchi Seas, the bluffs are receding up to 30 feet per storm," Bruce Molnia said. "They put boulders on the shoreline to protect it, and all of those got washed away. There used to be shoreline ice that no longer accumulates with the warming." That shoreline ice once buffered the shore from the storm surges.

Pam Miller of Arctic Connections in Anchorage said, "Standing along the shore of the Arctic Ocean you see big ice wedges just melting into muddy little rivulets that they make going out into the Beaufort Sea. You'll have this little cliff as the facade of the tundra hangs out with this carved-out area under it. It is like an overhang where it is melting out underneath it. For Alaska, there are changes. It is going to affect the infrastructure of villages, and the social investment of a lot of money."

Miller said a major change she has seen recently in Arctic Alaska is "the change due to coastal erosion, and the tremendous storms that occur along the Arctic Ocean coastline in the fall (August to October). Where in the past you had more sea ice near the shore, you can look out from the coastline of the Arctic Refuge and as far as you can see to the north is open water in September. And that is a major change. The scientific record shows that sea ice extent and thickness is dramatically changing in the Arctic. But it is something that you notice when you are standing there looking out from the coast. You can see where there has been coastal erosion from big storms.

"There is really a big bluff where the big ice wedges are just melting. And that has potential impacts for industrial infrastructure and oil field expansion. For example building buried sub-sea pipelines to the Northstar island, the question is whether they've taken into account how much that beach may erode over the 50-year lifespan of that field. There are a lot of questions about that."

CHAPTER TWELVE

Kivalina

Kivalina is a traditional Inupiat village located at the tip of an eight-mile barrier reef, between the Chukchi Sea and Kivalina River, 80 miles northwest of Kotzebue. Subsistence hunting forms the bulk of the protein of the people in Kivalina. Whitefish, salmon, seal, walrus, whale and caribou are all hunted for food and hides. The village has decided to relocate, in part because of the eroding beach that scientists say is likely being caused by global climate change.

"The reason we have to relocate is we are overcrowded on our little sand spit of an island, and we have no place to build anymore," said Kivalina Mayor Don Hawley. "There is no room to install sanitation facilities. We are surrounded on four sides with water. Our sanitation conditions in this village is totally third world. We are totally lacking sanitation facilities. We have to—for the good of our people—we need off this island.

"There's been erosion from natural conditions, from the spring melt-off and also from waves from the ocean. What the ocean is doing is getting more active. As far as waves are concerned, we are getting a lot more south-southwest winds. The waves are just eating away at the beach.

"On the lagoon side of this island, there's been a few people that have houses on the northeast side of the island. They have noticed that some of the spring melt-off has been eating away at the bank and it has been slowly closing in on their houses. But in the past the state and federal government have funded erosion control projects and they slowed down the pace of erosion."

Hawley said that eventually the airport will be next in line for erosion control because the airport is situated right on the spit. "If the waves keep coming like they have been, the airport will probably have to be addressed for erosion control. Once that happens, we'll seriously consider declaring an emergency."

Kivalina's average elevation is eight feet. With a population of 377, the village covers 1.9 square miles. A 1913 report by Northwest District Superintendent for the U.S. Department of Interior Walter Shields wrote a report on his visit to Kivalina when "the thermometer froze at—65 degrees so we do not know just how cold it was." Those temperatures that so characterized the Arctic for millennia no longer occur.

Hawley said the snowfall has "been varying by the years. Some years we will receive very little snowfall and other years we will receive a whole lot of snow. Once we receive a lot of snow, the spring melt-off will be heavy and when the melt-off is heavy, there is a chance that the erosion will be increased. But actually it has been varying by the years.

"Lately, like within the last ten years, snowfall has been heavier because of the warmer conditions. It seems like we're getting more low pressures and lots of moisture. What's happening is either we will get rain or snow when what we used to have was a good freeze and the rivers would be frozen solid and the ocean would be frozen solid. But lately the rivers have been real unstable and also the ocean.

"It's caused some concern, not only for the residents but also for what it has done to the animals. The animals that we rely on instead of being in the usual places where we find them they will move to different locations because the conditions are warmer." Global warming has totally changed the migration route of the fish and the ocean mammals, Hawley said.

"Currently the relocation (of the village) is under study. It has been that way since the relocation idea started back in the 80s. And so far all we are seeing is studies and more studies.

"There was a two-day storm that was moderately severe. Every fall there is a fall storm. In October 2002 it was moderately severe and it actually washed out one of our drain-field facilities. That was the only extent of erosion that we had there.

"But on the airport side, the airport manager has been noticing that the beach has been eroding at the pace of one foot every storm. With global warming lately we've been getting the storms periodically over the summer. But it used to be the spring and the sun we should have fair weather, sunshine and a little bit of rain. In the last part of August and September we'd get all the south winds. And that is when the storms happen; it used to be once a year. Now we're getting more and more precipitation: more rain, more south winds.

"The ocean is not freezing like it used to. And the rivers don't freeze like they used to. Last December, the river was free flowing. It only froze over in the last part of January. It affected the fish in the river—we couldn't find them.

"People realize that if the trend continues, the migration routes will probably change. There was one year when the spring melt-off was different. Some of the elders said this is the first time that we've seen the river do that ever."

CHAPTER THIRTEEN

Shishmaref

The villagers of Shishmaref plugged holes in their crumbling sea wall with sandbags ... to protect exposed permafrost from further erosion. A raging storm last week caused parts of the sea wall to crash into the Chukchi Sea, leaving homes literally teetering on the edge of the ocean embankment and exposing underlying permafrost to the sea. The warmer ocean waters have melted the permafrost, speeding up erosion," the Anchorage Daily News reported on October 9, 1997. The 1,300-foot wide barrier island is losing 25-125 feet in width every year.

Shishmaref is a Native American village located on the Bering Straight on the far western coast of Alaska, just 100 miles from Siberia. The village has a population of 590, with 136 families. Archaeologists found evidence that native peoples have lived there for centuries. The original Inupiat name for the island is Kigiktaq. In 1816, Lt. Otto Von Kotzebue named the inlet Shismarev after one of his crew. After 1900, a supply center was established there to supply gold mines, and the village was renamed after the inlet. But severe erosion that scientists have linked to global warming has caused homes to collapse into the sea, forcing the emergency movement of 20 homes, the building of a $110,000 sea wall and in time, officials say, the inevitable movement of the entire village. Villagers are worried that a gradual move will split the village, or worse that lack of funding might force people to move to other villages, abandoning Shishmaref.

The U.S. Army Corps of Engineers found that it would cost 102 million dollars to move the village from the barrier island where it currently resides to a hundred-acre area on the mainland. The General Accounting office reported that the cost may be as high as $400 million, and questioned whether it was worth the cost. The Corps of Engineers requires local communities to come up with 25-50% of the costs, something impossible for the village, and creating a dilemma that policy makers will increasingly need to deal with.

On July 20, 2002, the village of Shishmaref released the unofficial count of a vote to relocate the village. The vote was 161-20 in favor of moving. In January 2004 the village picked Tin Creek, 12 miles to the south, as the future site for the village. Tin Creek is near Ear Mountain, which villagers say can provide gravel for the new villages buildings, roads, airport, sewage lagoons and other development.

Shishmaref Lutheran Church Pastor Kim Oslovich said, "I've only lived here for six years but there has definitely been significant erosion over the course of those six years. There's significantly less shoreline, less beach, especially on the western side of the village. I think too that there has been some weather change. Everyone says that there has been some weather change. Even in the short time that I've been here, it seems like the fall storms are more severe and freeze-up tends to be a little later, things like that.

"The most obvious impact is more than 20 homes had to be moved from one part of the island to the other, and that was a major enterprise. The way it is now, the homes that were in imminent danger have all been moved. But right now there is a sea wall that is being constructed, so hopefully that will ameliorate some of our problems at least in the short-term, but as you know, holding back the ocean is not a thing you can really do. It is just a matter of time before we start losing land again.

Shishmaref is located on a sandy barrier island on Alaska's Chukchi Sea Coast, five miles from the Seward Peninsula mainland. It is near the Bering Land Bridge where native peoples and many animal species crossed into North America. "People have lived here for a long, long, long time," Oslivich said. "There are archeological digs that have found things that are really old, more than a thousand years old. But as far as a permanent settlement, that came into being when there was contact with European people, the Americans and Russians. And that would be in the mid to late 1800s.

"Erosion has been a consistent problem over the years. There was a particularly bad storm back in the early 70s that caused significant erosion. But I think the thing is it has definitely accelerated more in recent years, especially since 1997. We had a really bad storm in '97 that caused a huge amount of erosion, between 50 and 100 feet. That was when the first big batch of houses had to get moved. There were about 15 houses that were

Waves pound the western shore of Shishmaref where just a few years ago there was a wide beach. Photo by Tony Weyiouanna.

moved then. Since then, we have had more. Just last year we had significant erosion and three houses had to get moved.

"One of them had to have an emergency move 20 feet back because it got to the point where you would walk out the door and go right over the edge of the cliff. It was an October storm, and it really wasn't that bad of a storm," he said, estimating the wind speed at 30 knots. "It was not extreme weather, just bad enough and the wave action was with the winds the wrong way that it caused problems.

"It was dramatic. It was a dramatic loss of land. Before the storm there was a fairly wide beach. You could go down and drive on the beach on a four-wheeler. There was lots of space and people had their traditional drying racks for meat. After that the beach was just gone. The beach just disappeared. People lost a lot of meat that was on drying racks that got washed away.

"The governor declared a state of emergency. Houses were precarious on the edge of the bluff. It was pretty significant. One house that was very close to the edge that nobody was living in crashed over the bluff into the sea. I saw it sitting there at the bottom of the bluff when we came back, but then they cleaned it up. The bluff is probably 10 feet, 12 feet something like that.

"Tony (Weyiouanna) is kind of our point guy on this. He is kind of the lead guy on dealing with the different agencies, the different levels of government, and he's even gotten pretty good at dealing with the media. He's got tons of pictures."

A storm in November 2003 left five boats missing, including Weyiouanna's 22-foot plywood skiff, and forced the evacuation of five residents. Eight-foot waves chewed away at the bank, Weyiouanna reported. All the village lowlands were flooded and waves lapped the edges of the villages washing facilities and sewage lagoon.

"We have had a slew of people come up here to do stories on Shishmaref and most of them link it to global warming," Oslovich said. "We had the ABC affiliate in Anchorage come and do a story, we had the BBC from England come and do a story, Canadian Television, German television, the list is as long as your arm, and all of those people will ask people about climatic changes, especially elders.

"They will ask elders about climatic changes over the last 40-50 years. As people have reflected on these things, they will say you know, there does seem to be a correlation. It may well be that as things get warmer, the sea levels rise, the freeze-up is later. There is more damage from storms in the fall because the water is open for a longer period of time. I think some people are starting to make that connection over the last few years.

"We need to care for creation. If we don't care for it, we are all going to suffer. You see that on the micro-scale. You see that people around here traditionally only took what they needed from the land, and they used everything that they took, and that kind of balanced things out. And on the large scale, we do need to be concerned about those larger issues. And people around here are starting to think in those terms. They are starting to think in terms of how much pollution do the snow machines produce, and what kind of effect does that have. We'll see where that takes us.

"From June to October, we have open water. People do say that freeze-up has been later in the last few years. It's impacted people because of the physical effort of moving an entire home, and a bunch of homes. It really galvanized people to think about moving the whole village, because that has been kind-of floating in the air since that major storm back in the 70s, that maybe we should move.

"It is a barrier island and that might be a problem some day, having to physically move those houses because they were in imminent danger has really spurred people to get involved. We have public meetings about erosion and people go to them. There is interest and a drive that we do need to do something to protect our village."

CHAPTER FOURTEEN

Opening the Northwest Passage

With the thinning of polar ice, scientists have predicted the opening of the Northwest Passage to shipping in the near future. Already, non-ice breaking boats have navigated through in recent years. The passage has been open about 20 days a year, and scientists predict it will be open 100 days per year by 2050. Canada has claimed this territory as its own inland waters. The U.S. and many other countries, however, call it international waters, and do not intend to ask permission for passage.

The fabled Northwest Passage was originally sought as a trade route between Europe and China and India. Attempts to get around North America began in the 1490s with voyages by John Cabot that were unsuccessful. Cabot, with the support of many wealthy European merchants, believed there was a passage to Asia going west. When reports came back in 1493 that Christopher Columbus had (erroneously) reached Asia, Cabot began work on a direct passage through the north. In 1496 he got approval and funding from King Henry VII of England.

He set sail from Bristol on 1497, going generally northwest. After a rough crossing of the Atlantic, he sailed along the Labrador, Newfoundland and New England coasts. He thought the land was in northeastern Asia, and claimed the area for the King. He returned with a group of four ships and about 300 people. He reached Greenland and sailed north until his crew mutinied because of the severe cold. He was forced to return to England because he was so low on supplies, and died shortly thereafter.

Sir John Franklin was a decorated war veteran for England, and had extensive experience in explorations of the Arctic regions of Canada and Alaska. In 1845 he left with a crew of 129 and two boats, the Terror and the Erebus. The ships were last seen by a whaling vessel in Baffin Bay on July 26, 1845. Ships were sent to find them from 1848 to 1859. Franklin's second wife outfitted an expedition in 1847—the Fox—that finally found the remnants of the expedition. The ships had become locked in ice in September 1846 between Victoria Island and King William Island. Franklin and others died, and the crew deserted the ships in 1848, only to die in the frigid northern lands.

The existence of the Northwest Passage was proven in 1854, and Roald Amundsen finally made the passage from the Atlantic to the Pacific from 1903 to 1906. During this expedition, he determined the position of the north magnetic pole. In 1969, the U.S. icebreaker the Manhattan became the first large ship to make the northern sea route.

Colin Nickerson wrote in the Boston Globe, March 21, 2000 that, "The rapid retreat of the ice is also opening the way to direct challenges to Canada's control over the waters of its vast northern realms—above all, its claim to the legendary Northwest Passage." Nickerson described the area as one of the most sensitive environmental zones and a critical strategic arena. The Northwest Passage refers to numerous different passages through the northern territories.

Weller said "The opening of the northwest and northeast sea routes will allow the possibility of ship traffic through the Arctic Ocean: a distance much shorter and much more economical. But this ship traffic could also increase pollution with tanker traffic."

The issue has been a sore point between U.S. and Canada, with the commander of the Canadian forces of the far north saying it may need to use firepower to enforce its claims over the 1.5 million square miles of northern ocean terrain.

In August 1999, Inuit fishermen were surprised by a submarine that surfaced right next to them. By the time Canada's patrol planes reached the area, the sub had submerged. The

Inuit reported more sub sightings in the next few weeks. The Canadian government thinks that the sub was likely French or American based on descriptions of it from the Inuit. Canada's head of ice breaking operations predicted in 2000 that there was no question that the Northwest Passage would open, the question is whether it would be in a few years or decades.

CHAPTER FIFTEEN

Movin' on Up
Animals and Plants Migrate North

As the climate warms, the northern limit of the animal and plant specie moves farther north. As specie move into areas where previously they have not been, they are creating a massive change in the ecology with predictions of the end of the tundra in Alaska.

"Fisheries are a big part of Alaska. We export a lot. Effects of climate change on fisheries could be quite dramatic too," Guntner Weller said. "We have seen diverging evidence of impacts. It is clear that ocean temperatures have an impact on the distribution of fish. They are very sensitive. Fish are displaced and new species come in. This could mean a relocation of infrastructure. The biggest fishing ports are Kodiak and Dutch Harbor (Alaska Peninsula). The fishing ports may need to change. It is a huge impact on fish supplies for the U.S.

"We see evidence of exotic species—animals that have not been seen before in these regions. The natives tell us that they see bird species they have no name for because they have never seen them before. This includes big land mammals. In Seward Peninsula, we see beavers. We see moose on the North Slope (of the Brooks Mountain Range). We see bigger stands of willows. So there is a shift in animals."

"As the trees and bushes march north over what was once tundra, so do beavers, and they are damming new rivers and lakes, to the detriment of water quality and, possibly, salmon eggs," reported Yereth Rosen on April 21, 2004.

A $6 million documentary series on global warming's impact on the Arctic, Arctic Mission by writer-producer Jean Lemire filmed the new arrival of robins, ants, grizzly bears and moose; they have been seen in the Arctic for the first time recently because of global warming. The program ran in Canada on David Suzuki's

The Nature of Things. Suzuki said that Inuit children have been afraid of dragonflies, which they had not seen before.

Gwich'in Moses Lord of Fort Yukon also reported seeing different animals. "There are a few different birds around. There are a few cougars spotted—at least three times. Black cougar were spotted. We noticed the caribou are confused. They go in different groups. They are not all together (in a single group) like a long time ago."

Arctic Village Elder Sarah James said climate change is reducing berry harvests. "During the summertime, sometimes cold spells will come and that is not good for berries, or the animals. One year there were no berries. Bear got really aggressive because they did not have the berries for food. And that goes for all the animals that depend on the berries. When that happens, they get attracted to human trash, and they become a nuisance for the village.

"Arctic Village—that used to be the tree line. We used to be nomadic. The creek was called the creek with high banks. It was a popular stopover because that used to be one of the favorite places to set fish traps. That was the tree line, but now the tree line is past the Brooks Range. The tree line is on the North side of the Brooks Range." Arctic Village is on the south side of the Brooks Mountains.

"We never used to have cottonwood. Now we have miniature cottonwood. We never used to have beaver or black bear. The last few years we see black bear. The black bear live with wood. Woodchuck and woodpecker come in— we never used to see them. Hawks and different kinds of birds come in. It was mainly open country before but there is more vegetation coming in." The lake by the airport in which I had caught a large northern pike during my first visit to Arctic Village was pretty well drained, she reported.

So much vegetation has grown into the creeks that it has eliminated the travel of fish, James said. "It blocks the fish in the creeks."

An increase in beaver populations and their moving north into areas they previously have not been have also been reported to block fish from reaching their spawning grounds. Paul Erhart, from Tanana said, "We now have more beaver than ever in this slough because of warm winters that give the beaver the most favorable conditions to survive. (Beaver) then proceed to dam and tier off the sloughs so resident species of fish, which again provides the Indians with a very viable source of food, cannot reach their spawning ground to provide the next generation of food for the Indians of the Interior."

Red fox have moved up to 600 miles north and established themselves in areas formerly dominated by the Arctic Fox, the Pew Center on Global Climate Change reported in Novermber, 2004. While the Arctic Fox is better adapted to cold, in direct fights between red and Arctic fox, red fox will prevail. The red fox is not as adapted to the cold as the Arctic Fox, with longer ears and limbs that lose more heat. But as the climate has warmed so drastically in the Arctic, the red fox has moved far north. Scientists say the two species cannot co-exist.

On Baffin Island in far northeast Canada, the red fox has moved 600 miles north in 30 years. As the red fox marched north, the Arctic fox retreated north, either due to warming, competition with the red fox, or both, the Pew Center reported. With the projection of a continuation of warming trends, the range of the Arctic fox will be further reduced. Scientists found that the red fox moved farther north in areas that warmed more. The Pew Center report found that in the Arctic, most regions have experienced a temperature increase of 4 to 7 degrees in the last 50 years.

Williams confirmed that species are moving north. "We are finding tuna where they have never been in Alaska. Species are now showing up that were not here before because it is warmer. The shrub line has dramatically marched north.

"The reason that Alaska was the place where it was predicted to warm the most and has warmed the most is that in the lower 48 as the temperature goes from 69 to 70 or 69 to 72, well it is warmer but it is not a profound tipping point. In Alaska, when the temperature goes from 31 to 33 and you go from a temperature at which you create ice and snow to a temperature where you create rain and brown, that has a profound impact and accelerating impacts.

"With the vegetation marching north, not only does that change the vegetation, you have animals following that vegetation, such as moose on the North Slope where they had never been seen before.

"Moose have only reached out on the north slope in the 20th century, since about mid century," said scientist Dr. Glenn Juday. "In the mid 50s people began to report them. Now they are well established with the improvement of the habitat with the establishment of the tall shrubs that is their food source. That is likely caused by the warming."

"Every once in a while you experience something that seems very aberrant," Williams said. "I was on the Trustee council for the Exxon Valdez oil spill. And we were going around an island in Prince William Sound because we were looking at using some of the settlement money between Exxon Valdez and the state of Alaska to buy Afognak Island. We went to this one bay and it was filled with substantially over a hundred, somewhere between a hundred and two hundred salmon sharks.

"Salmon sharks are thriving in the warmer water. I've only seen a handful of salmon sharks in my 23 years in Alaska. And to just go in this bay and see potentially over a hundred salmon shark fins in this bay, it was breathtaking in a very negative way." Salmon sharks threaten the thriving salmon fisheries in Alaska that have evolved largely without their predation.

Wohlforth found that the different distributions of animals made hunting more difficult and different than it traditionally was for Inupiat peoples. Also, as the permafrost melts, this adds more nutrients to the Arctic waterways, making them more like temperate waters, he said.

"There is some research going on at Atuvik Lake field camp about what happens when you greatly increase the nutri-

The author caught these two 30 pound salmon during his July 2004 summer tour of the old growth forest in southeast Alaska (the subject of an upcoming book). With their spawning streams warming rapidly, salmon shark populations soaring and warm-water parasites eating away at their muscle tissue, the fate of the salmon, a weathervane of the health of our planet, is uncertain. Photo by Joe Jensen.

ents in the stream," Wohlforth said. "Because when you have the thawing permafrost going into the stream, you have a lot of nutrients being released into that water. And what they found is kind of what you would expect, the streams become much more productive, more fish, moss and grass, stuff like that. It is more like a stream in the temperate climate. But as to what the impact of that is, they are speculating. A lot of research shows that the biological ranges are moving northward." The big question is what will happen to the specie that live in the far north: the Arctic Char, Dolly Varden, Grayling, Burbout and others as their Arctic habitat changes more temperate.

"Hunting is the essence of their culture," Wohlforth said of the Inupiat. "As the climate changes, it forces changes on the environment which forces changes on them and I think that is the most important thing. There are changes in the berry picking activities, a lot of that is documented.

The North Sea is undergoing an ecological meltdown caused by global warming, scientists reported in October 2003. Scientists report a "collapse in the system." Record water temperatures are killing the plankton that forms the base of the food chain, causing fish and bird populations to drop rapidly. The warm temperatures have driven cold-water species hundreds of miles north. Catches of salmon and cod are down and the size of the fish is smaller as well. Scientists predict that cod will become extinct in the North Sea in the next few decades.

While over-fishing caused much of the initial decline, scientists expected a major rebound with the reduction in fishing quotas, but they have not been seen, and global warming appears to be the reason why. With this elimination of the base of the food chain, many species are affected, including birds and dolphins. The Royal Society for the Protection of Birds concluded from its research that seabird colonies of kttiwakes, puffins and razorbills off the coast of Yorkshire and the Shetlands in 2003 suffered their worst breeding season since records began, with many birds abandoning their nests. Eels have been hard hit as well.

The numbers of salmon have dropped by half in 20 years in the North Sea. Salmon are highly dependent on plankton on their journey to feeding areas in the north Atlantic. Sand eels, which make up a third to half of the weight of all fish in the North Sea have also remarkably declined. In 2003, the Danish fleet caught only 300,000 tons of its 950,000-ton quota, a record low.

CHAPTER SIXTEEN

Locking Horns with Climate Change
The Caribou Challenge

Fran Mauer warned that a forested north slope, as Glen Juday predicts if current trends continue, would be a drastic change for all tundra wildlife, in many cases threatening their continued existence in those areas. "It would be really different than it is today and has been over the time period that we are familiar with. It is hard to fathom the whole thing. What would it be like if there was a forest on the North Slope. The relationship between predators and prey would be vastly different. Northern migratory caribou herds: a big part of their behavior and their migrations is based on the open terrain that they live in and their ability to see and detect predators from a distance. All that strategy would not work well in a forest situation.

"We do have caribou in North America that live in forests and we call them woodland caribou and they behave much differently. They don't travel in big massive herds. They behave more like white tailed deer on a spectrum of behavioral characteristics. The caribou phenomenon as we know it today would be very different if it were mostly forested. I can't see the forests going high in the Brooks Range to the tops of the mountains in the near future by any means, so there would be some higher elevation tundra areas more fragmented and separated by forested valleys so conceivably there may be smaller less migratory isolated subpopulations of caribou scattered in the Brooks Range.

"That is similar to what we see in southern Alaska, where we don't have any large migratory herds in southern Alaska, they are relatively small, isolated herds. And many of those herds are declining. Some of them have declined dramatically and are endangered."

Mauer said that caribou have been acting differently since the late 1980s, spending less time on the coastal plain and in two remarkable years they calved prior to reaching the coastal plain.

"Why the calving didn't occur in the Arctic coastal plain in 2000 and 2001," Mauer said, "may or may not be related to climate change or global warming. What happened in both years was there was a very late onset of spring, and a fairly deep snow on the winter range and along the migration route northward. The migration of pregnant females was delayed by as much as a month. The deep snow further slowed them down in moving north. They tend to not move until there is definite melting underway. If there is cold inclement weather during migration, a lot of them stop moving.

"That is the kind of conditions that occurred in 2000 and 2001. We had the extreme case of caribou not making it onto the Arctic coastal plain coming out of the Canadian winter ranges primarily and having calving scattered along the migration route and off in the Canadian region. We saw an extreme in that pattern. We've seen that kind of thing in other years where the spring is late, but not as pronounced as what we saw in 2000 and 2001 where there were even a few cows that were born south of the Porcupine River which we had never seen before in 30 years of monitoring caribou there."

Mauer said there was "extreme late snowmelt. I wouldn't say necessarily record deep snow but deep snow on the migration route. Now whether that is due to some global warming connection I have no idea. Some people would say well that certainly is no sign of warming, we have later springs and slow melting conditions. But this whole business is very complicated, and we may see extremely different patterns than we are used to but not always warmer conditions."

Alaska Coalition Outreach Coordinator Dan Ritzman said that the great increase in mortality during those years accentuates the importance of protecting the Arctic Refuge coastal plain from oil development. Should development be permitted, caribou would likely avoid those areas as they have around Prudhoe Bay. This would push them to calve into the areas that caused such a great increase in mortality.

Mauer concurred that there are similarities between how oil development would impact the caribou. "Yes they did have higher mortality of calves in those years. If there is oil field development, the caribou will get there, but once they get there they will shy away from the development zone and have to seek alternate places, often going near to the mountains.

"The problem is the oil field development would be there year after year after year, and it would be a permanent loss of calving area. Whereas the extreme weather conditions of 2000 and 2001 have swung back in the last couple years. It was an extreme example of what we could expect, but it is not exactly the same.

"In other years when caribou are late, the whole herd still moves onto the coastal plain. Another difference with the weather phenomenon in 2000 and 2001 is it is a good thing they did not make it to the coastal plain because it was covered in snow. The caribou adjusted to avoid going out on the snowy coastal plain. They at least gave birth to their calves where the snow was melting."

If the caribou are squeezed toward the mountains by oil development, this would cause an increased predation on calves and a decrease in food supply, Mauer said, both of which would negatively affect the Porcupine Caribou Herd. "There is a greater risk of predation. Wolves have their dens on the northern mountain valleys, not on the coastal plain. Most of the bears den in the mountain foothills, not on the plain. Up near the mountains there are more golden eagle nests. When you add all those up, it puts the calves in closer proximity to predators. So we expect there would be a greater loss of young calves when they are the most vulnerable. In studies in the early 80s, we found a great risk to calves that spent time near the mountains.

This photo shows tens of thousands of caribou massing on the coastal plain of the Arctic National Wildlife Refuge to give birth to the next generation of caribou. Photo courtesy of the Alaska Coalition

"Also, if they are squeezed to the mountains, there is more of a limitation of food. Their options of food are more constrained in that they can't go out in the plain following the plant chronology. That will likely result in a slower growth rate of calves and influence the health of the calves."

The winter of 2003 showed a normal calving season that can, hopefully, in the midst of the added attack of climate change, ensure the survival of the caribou. It is symbolic and ironic that the caribou are being attacked on both fronts in this last frontier in the last corner of America. Climate change and oil development are related and are both threatening the survival of the greatest nomadic land animal on earth.

"The other thing that we have seen in recent years is the shortening of the length of time that the Porcupine Caribou Herd spends on the coastal plain of the Arctic National Wildlife Refuge," Mauer said. "Back in the mid 1980s and up to about 1990, it wasn't uncommon for caribou to stay on the coastal plain to the very end of June and sometimes well into July.

"Starting for sure in 1995 to the present time, the Porcupine herd has spent less time on the costal plain and migrated south into the mountains and east into Canada sometimes around the

22nd of June, so probably a good week or 10 days earlier than the pattern we were seeing in the early 80s. One of the things that the climatologists talk about is unpredictable or different patterns from what people are used to seeing.

"It seems like the types of weather that stimulate caribou to leave the coastal plain is frequently when there is a cold storm front that moves across the plain from the west to east or from the northwest to east, and usually there is snow associated with it. When they are calving, generally the caribou will move south toward the mountains, and if the weather persists, they often will continue further south and east through the mountains and not come back to the coastal plain.

"Sometimes if it is a brief event they will move a little ways into the mountains then if the weather moderates in a day or two they will come back out on the plain. But lately they've just been moving in and leaving, so we end up with probably a week to ten days earlier evacuation of the caribou from the refuge coastal plain than what we were seeing in the 80s.

"It seems to be associated with cold fronts moving in from the west that stimulates that movement. It is very complicated. One of the things that happens when those cold events comes through is it retards or knocks down the emergence and abundance of mosquitoes. So during those years, caribou are able to move south ultimately into a better range for food.

"It is different, and how well they are able to adjust to it, I don't think anyone has a solid answer to that. It certainly is different. For whatever it is worth, the Porcupine Caribou herd has been in a declining trend. That trend began at the end of the 1980s, which was about the same time that we began to see this different movement pattern on the coastal plain. Whether they are related or not, I have no idea. There are many things that can influence the population level.

"The last time the count was done was 2001 and there were 123,000 caribou counted on aerial photos. The peak count was in 1989 when 187,000 were counted. So it is a drop of more than 60,000 in twelve years.

"The population may be influenced by climate change, but how much and what other factors are involved are complicated. The weather up there since I began coming up there myself is highly variable to begin with, so it is not easy to just flat out say yeah, this is definitely different. It is my impression that the onset of winter conditions and cold weather is later now than it was 25-30 years ago, whereas the onset of spring has not necessarily come earlier, looking at it from a caribou perspective."

Mauer said that though the caribou may stay on the coastal plain for a shorter period of time, that does not diminish the need to protect the plain from oil development. "As long as caribou do go on the coastal plain, we ought to remember why they are going there. The main thing they do is give birth to their calves. From a vulnerability standpoint to the calves, this is the most critical time. It is when calves are incapable of defending from predators. As long as caribou are going there to give birth to their calves, it is going to remain a serious issue if it is open to drilling."

Caribou on the coastal plain.

CHAPTER SEVENTEEN

Feedback Loops

The albeido effect is the amount of light that the Earth absorbs from the sun. The white polar ice and snowy Arctic tundra reflects most of the sun's energy back to space, while open water and vegetation absorb most of that energy, creating what scientists call a feedback loop, where global warming causes further warming.

Dr. Comiso said "this is a major effect in the Arctic region. If you look at the different regions, that is why the Arctic and Antarctic are so different. In the Antarctic, you have a big continent there called Antarctica, greater than the size of the United States and Alaska combined, and that's always covered by snow, so the continent is high. In the summer, when the sea ice retreats, the sea ice cover is reduced to about 25 percent of the winter ice cover. The impact of the sea ice retreat is not quite the impact as in the Arctic, because in the Arctic, what you have as a reflector of solar radiation is the sea ice cover. Greenland is quite small compared to Antarctica. Just sea ice cover and Greenland together are the only entities in the Arctic that reflect solar energy and keeps a lot of heat from being absorbed by the Earth.

"Now as the ice retreats, and what we have observed recently is that the summer sea ice is retreating quite rapidly at the rate of 9 to 10 percent per decade. As that ice retreats, you have less and less of that reflector in the Arctic. During the peak of summer for example when you have 24 hours a day of solar radiation, as you get less and less ice there, then you get more and more solar radiation to the Arctic Ocean. As the Arctic Ocean gets warmer, then the impact there is the freeze up of sea ice is later and later, and the melt-off of sea ice comes sooner as well. You have longer periods of melt, and therefore you have thinner ice. Which then becomes even more vulnerable to melting, so this is what we have been calling feedback.

"There is certainly something going on in the region. I think that there has to be a concern. Especially since because there are these various feedbacks that I have been talking about. Like if you look in the summer if you look at the perennial ice, and all of the radiation from the sun, and you see the large fraction that would be absorbed by the ocean, so I don't know. Climate in the Arctic can certainly be affected.

"What happens is when you have less ice you will have more exposed ocean. Then you're replacing high-albeido ice with low-albeido ocean, so you melt your ice early in these shallow seas in the Arctic, and you have sun shining on them that could warm up that water quite a bit. So then what you expect is in the fall when the ice starts to grow again it just takes a lot longer because now it has to cool down that ocean that has warmed up quite a bit in the summertime because it was exposed to the sun and less was reflected back by the ice cover.

"The ocean absorbs more sunlight. The ocean ends up warming up because the seas are fairly shallow all around the Arctic edge. So each year this continues to happen you may get a point where there is no sea ice.

"We're using these models where the mechanisms are fairly complicated because now if we melt the ice and then the ocean is exposed then what does that mean if there is more cloudiness. So suddenly you get a lot more cloudiness and these low-level clouds will reflect sunlight also. So maybe it won't warm up in the ocean as much because now you have this cloud affect. So we unravel each of these mechanisms, but in the end what we need to figure out is which of these mechanisms end up winning."

Changing open tundra to forest greatly increases the amount of energy that the Earth absorbs, says Williams. "The vegetation does change the albeido. Alaska vegetation in particular, like the black spruce, is well adapted to absorb heat. It is very dark and absorbs a lot of heat. When you push black spruce and other vegetation north, you have this positive feedback where it accelerates the impacts of global warming. So it is quite extraordinary."

Scientific findings in 2004 show that Arctic ice absorbs carbon dioxide, meaning the loss of ice will create yet another feedback loop as this mechanism for reducing this greenhouse gas in the atmosphere is lost as the ice melts.

CHAPTER EIGHTEEN

Chill Out

How Global Warming May Make the North Atlantic Cooler

Earth's oceans play a major role in regulating the global temperatures of the planet. Each ocean has a circulating deep ocean current that moves cooler and warmer water to different parts of the globe. Scientists are finding that this thousand mile wide ocean current is very complex and very sensitive to temperature and other climatic changes. The melt-off of fresh water in the Arctic may shut down the North Atlantic Oscillation that brings warmer tropical water to Europe and the northeastern United States, keeping England, which is in the same latitude as Labrador about ten degrees F. warmer.

Raymond Schmitt, a Senior Scientist in the Department of Physical Oceanography at the Woods Hole Oceanographic Institution said in 2000, "the crucial role of the oceans in climate has not been sufficiently acknowledged in most research on climate change to date, including the National Climate Assessment Report under discussion here. It was a tradition of the climate modeling community to treat the ocean as a shallow swamp; a source of moisture, but playing no role in heat transport and storage. We now know this to be a significant error, the oceans are an equal partner with the atmosphere in transporting heat from the equator to the poles, and a reservoir of heat and water that overwhelmingly dwarfs the capacity of the atmosphere."

Schmitt outlined facts about The Oceans impact on global weather. Oceans:

• "Cover 70% of the surface of the Earth.

- "Have 1,100 times the heat capacity of the atmosphere (99.9% of the heat capacity of the Earth's fluids)

- "Contain 90,000 times as much water as the atmosphere (97% of the free water on the planet)

- "Receive 78% of global precipitation"

As salty water in the north Atlantic gives off its heat, from having traveled from tropical areas, it sinks. This pulls warmer surface water from the south, creating the North Atlantic Oscillation that has a massive impact on temperatures around the Atlantic. Schmitt said that this effect, called "thermohaline circulation," is far greater than the amount of water moved through evaporation and precipitation, and is the largest source of ocean transportation of heat from the tropics to the Arctic. This effect, also called an ocean conveyer, helps to pull the warmer Gulf Stream waters into the north Atlantic. The slow current moves more than a hundred times the amount of water as the Amazon River, warming Europe by about 18 degrees Fahrenheit. This effect helps to moderate winter conditions throughout the north Atlantic region.

Scientists measure the ocean currents with drifting monitors like weather balloons that flow with the current then rise to the surface to report salinity and temperature data to satellites. Then they drift another 10 days, repeating this up to 150 times. They have found that it is slowing down. Scientists report that the ocean circulation has slowed by about 20 percent, the *Seattle Post Intelligencer* reported April 16, 2004.

If the waters of the North Atlantic become too fresh from the melting of glaciers and increased precipitation, the water may not sink, shutting down the oscillation. Schmitt reports that this has happened before. The most recent one occurred about 12,000 years ago, he said, with very dramatic consequences on the northern hemisphere, returning much if it to glacial conditions for a thousand years. Fossil records indicate that this happened in only 10-20 years. The temperatures of the

North Atlantic were five degrees Celsius (nine degrees Fahrenheit) cooler than previously.

Ruth Curry, a research specialist in the WHOI Physical Oceanography Department, Bob Dickson of the Center for Environment, Fisheries, and Aquaculture Science in Lowestoft, United Kingdom, and Igor Yashayaev of the Bedford Institute of Oceanography in Dartmouth, Nova Scotia, Canada released a study in December, 2003 that found a significant increase in salinity in the tropics, and a decrease in salinity in areas of higher latitudes, indicating it may not be long before the North Atlantic Oscillation shuts down.

In addition to the overwhelming weight of evidence for this phenomenon, NASA reported in April, 2004 that they had found a slow-down of the North Atlantic Oscillation in the late 1990s from analyses of satellite data. Co-author of the study Peter Rhines warned that what happens in the North Atlantic affects global weather patterns. "It's like Grand Central Station there, as many of the major ocean water masses pass through from the Arctic and from warmer latitudes," he said. The North Atlantic Oscillation, also called a subpolar gyre, can take 20 years to complete its cycle. Warm water runs north through the Gulf Stream, past Ireland, before it turns west near Iceland and the tip of Greenland.

It is a paradox that global warming may cause a little ice age in the northern hemisphere, and one that right-wing propagandists for the status quo fossil fuel industry lobby will likely twist to discredit climate change. And it is why the issue is better termed climate change than global warming. On average, globally, temperatures are and will undoubtedly warm as more and more greenhouse gases are pumped into the atmosphere. But locally, the complex weather patterns can cause cooling of some areas and warming of others.

A paper coauthored by Terrence Joyce, Senior Scientist, Physical Oceanography and Lloyd Keigwin, Senior Scientist, Geology & Geophysics found that "Evidence for abrupt climate change is readily apparent in ice cores taken from Greenland and Antarctica." Joyce and Keigwin wrote that the North Atlantic Oscillation, "heat engine operates to reduce equator-to-pole temperature differences and is a prime moderating mechanism for climate on Earth." Fresh water from glacial melt-off can stop or reduce the effect of this mechanism.

The two scientists wrote, "Recent evidence shows that the high latitude oceans have freshened while the subtropics and tropics have become saltier. These possible changes in the hydrological cycle have not been limited to the North Atlantic... We begin to approach how the paradox mentioned above can happen: Global warming can induce a colder climate for many of us." Another impact of this oscillation is by increasing precipitation over the poles, where it stores as glacial ice, affecting the hydrology of the planet. Shutting it off might lower this precipitation, thus decreasing the amount of snow accumulating as glacial ice over the North Pole.

CHAPTER NINETEEN

Alaska's Dying Forests

Just as scientists have predicted, climate change has caused the dying and drying forests of Alaska to burn in ever-greater intensity. In the summer of 2004, fires burned a record six million acres of forest in Alaska, much of it attributed to the fact the forests have died because of climate change. Even way up in the Yukon in Old Crow, a smoky haze limited the view in August 2004.

Flying from Arctic Village to Fairbanks I saw the forests on fire, billowing up thick clouds of smoke from the roaring blazes. There were many fires going, and we could see large areas of blackened earth where they had passed through. The turbulence was intense, shaking the little plane about. As we neared Fairbanks, the smoke was so intense we could not see anything.

Winds shook the plane as we came in for the landing. I could not see anything but thick gray smoke. We came down real fast, shaking about. Once outside, the smoke was intense and it hurt my lungs. Backpacking around Fairbanks, I knew at once I had to escape. Though wanting to walk about and interview people around Fairbanks, I called up a friend from college who had a cabin with an air purifier near the city and retreated from the lung damaging smog.

With millions of acres of spruce forest having died recently across southern Alaska, scientists have found human-caused climate change to be the cause. Scientist Glen Juday reported that he has found a temperature, 16 degrees Celsius, at which when achieved and exceeded, tree growth declines rapidly. This temperature had previously been quite rare, but with climate change has become more common at the expense of the forest.

Juday has been studying the reasons behind the massive die-out of trees in southern Alaska, as well as what the future will be for the northern landscape. "I am part of the long-term ecological research group at the Bonanza Creek. I have been doing long-term ecological research in general for many years," he said. "And in particular I do tree ring research. I use the tree-ring technique to look at these things.

In looking at the growth of trees in the boreal forest region of Alaska, we know one thing for many decades, we know that the trees in particularly sensitive locations, such as trees in the tree line are under a real close control by the climate. In good years they grow a whole lot more than poor years. So this relationship is so good that you can actually use the tree rings to reconstruct the past climates. The classic way of doing that is to look at the ring width, to see how much growth there was.

"But there are other techniques, like carbon 13 isotope content of the wood year by year. That goes up and down with changes in the environment. And finally the density of the wood as measured by X-Ray means. So we've used all three of these techniques. We looked at several white spruce on our most productive upland sites in the boreal region," he explained, noting it was outside the flood plain.

We found that contrary to what we expected, the trees grew the least in the warmest years, and they grew the most in the coolest summers. That just moves exactly the opposite of what people had expected. And in fact what they have established for many tree line trees, which go way up to the edge of the tree line in the mountains or north near the edge of the tree line, where a warm year it would grow better and a cool year it wouldn't grow much.

"We used that data to reconstruct past climates," Juday said. "When we tried that much further south and lower in elevation, and the really productive boreal white spruce stands that are in and around central Alaska, we found just the opposite compared to the tree-line trees. And not only that, but we have climate records from the Fairbanks Research Station, from about 1906 onward, so we have most of the twentieth century.

When we looked, we found that the last couple of decades in the century were the warmest summers and sustained. And that was the period where the trees grew the worst, and by far, quite a bit.

"Now we have begun to extend that research. I just had a PhD Student, Martin Vilkey who put together a big data set on the Brooks Range, along with some cores from the Alaska Range, and another Master's student Herald Zault, who did work in the Alaska Range. We had a massive sample, a big sample with more than 1,400 trees cored. We had 13 sites, and two mountain ranges so it is really reliable results. We found that contrary again to what we expected, about 40 percent of the trees at or near the tree line were the same negative responders. Warm summers had poor growth. You could actually predict their growth just by the July temperature. Warm July poor growth, cool July, good growth.

"We found that a little less than 40 percent were positive responders. Only they responded to the early temperatures, like April or March. When you had a warm March/April, good growth, and cool March/April, poor growth. So now we have a picture of the trees growing in our coldest environments and showing that nearly half of them are also negative responders. And we went one step further to show that the negative effect isn't produced until the temperature reaches a certain threshold. It turned out to be a July temperature average of about 16 degrees Celsius.

"When the temperature was colder than 16 degrees Celsius at Fairbanks, it got some production but it was pretty weak with the growth of these negative responders. But boy after 16 degrees their growth went way down, a real tight relationship. And that indicates that there is a threshold affect. So as it gets warmer during these critical time periods for their growth, it really subtracts from that growth. It turned out that again, in fact we split the twentieth century in half, and showed there were significant predicted relationships before 1950, but after 1950, they were real strong. The difference was simply that after 1950, we had a lot of these years of warm summers. It is really reducing the growth of the trees on our sites.

"We went one step further and extended that work to black spruce, paper birch, and found both had negative responders. We found a lot of negative responders to paper birch. We are kind of filling out the picture now by region and species and responder types. And we are finding that a substantial number of trees in our forest are being reduced in the amount of growth they can achieve because of warm temperatures. The warm temperatures have become more common. Finally, there is some threshold temperatures. Where it is warmer than those, growth is really reduced. Since that is a straight-line relationship, we've taken the climate change scenarios that have been run for the 21st century; five different climate scenarios. We used those scenarios to see what would happen.

"Because there was a straight line relationship, we found that several of the negative responding species site types during that 21st century scenario period got warm enough that the relationship showed zero growth.

"With these scenarios, then these species will not be able to grow anymore during the warmer times. The second issue is, wait a minute. If you stress some of your house plants, for example if you don't water them, they can get so weak that you come back on vacation, and you water them but they go ahead and die. It is the same thing in the wild. If you stress a plant badly enough, two things happen. It can reach a pivotal stage short of the zero line that I am talking about, where the temperatures are so high that growth is zero according to the predictions. Clearly the plant will probably kick the bucket sometime before you get there."

CHAPTER TWENTY

Heat Wave

Guntner Weller said climate change has caused large infestations of parasite disease species like the spruce bark beetle in southeast Alaska that have laid waste to unprecedented large areas of forest, destroying millions of acres of spruce. "That is undoubtedly caused by a warmer climate," the scientist said.

Tom Moran reported in the Fairbanks Daily News-Miner that the forests in Alaska have been thinning out. More heat but the same amount of available water, is stressing trees, making them more susceptible to insects such as bark beetles. The Christian Science Monitor reported on June 12, 2001 that scientists estimate that a third to a half of all the white spruce in Alaska have been killed in just 15 years. Meanwhile, in northern Alaska, shrubs are growing larger and are spreading north into areas of the tundra that have been barren for millennia.

On the Kenai Peninsula, more than four million acres of spruce forest have died because spruce bark beetles have attacked the global warming-weakened trees, federal scientists report. Timothy Egan wrote in the New York Times, "Century-old spruce trees stand silvered and cinnamon-colored as they bleed sap."

"In Fairbanks and other places, the bugs normally go south (or hibernate) but now they stay all winter," Sarah James said. "There are strange bugs like the beetles that are killing the spruce trees. The spruce beetles are mainly south of Fairbanks, but it will probably get to our village as it gets warmer," the elder predicted.

"One of the most moving things when I was up in Fairbanks for the original climate change conference proceedings in the mid 90s was that Juday took some of us out to the experimental biological station," Williams said. "There were a couple chunks of forest that they have been monitoring over a long time, and they talked about the impacts that were being seen then and they were quite dramatic. The impacts that are being seen now are horrifying. You go and you see the disease factor.

"I think when most Americans think about global warming, they might imagine glaciers melting, and ice caps. That is something that has a clear cause and effect. I think that the stories that have not been told well yet, I think in general but particularly in Alaska, are the increase in disease vectors and disease vectors that global warming enhances.

"I think the disease and insect and other secondary impacts of global warming are the scariest. And what you see when you go up to Fairbanks with the forest is global warming's impact in fostering spruce bark beetle propagation and fostering spruce bug worm and fostering birch leaf minor and aspen leaf minor. And you go to these forests and you stand on this one cliff and you look over at the larch and Juday said that 80 to 90 percent of Alaska's larch stands died through disease related with global warming. And you just look at these huge dead stands of larch trees.

"A story that has been covered better is the spruce bark beetle infestation in south-central Alaska. But it is compelling that the larch story hasn't. Then you look at the spruce bud worm, and you see the tips of the magnificent white spruce curled up and diseased. And you look at the leaf minors, the aspen and birch and this is a devastated forest. Glen Juday says that he doesn't think if climate change continues that white spruce forests will be in existence in Alaska. They will be gone, gone. This whole forest ecosystem will be gone."

Juday said, "The other thing that happens is those warm temperatures are often the key environmental trigger for natural disturbance agents—insects especially because in a cool boreal region, warm temperatures previously have been limiting, so the insects and their life history strategy of low population background levels until that infrequent warm summers and then that warmth is the signal and their populations go on a big upswing and they have big outbreaks and they attack and kill trees. That is a natural process that the boreal forest is well adapted to."

"What we appear to be confronting is through climate warming that outbreak level of some of the insect agents that can kill trees is coming more frequently, more severely over greater areas and is becoming itself a factor that one could project would completely change forest types over large landscapes. And in fact we have an example of that in the Kenai Peninsula and the whole south-central Alaska spruce bark beetle system.

"Based on what we know, if we have climates similar to the scenarios that were produced, that if it were that much warmer, well short of the point of no growth, you could have stress mortality on a huge scale just from insect outbreaks that are triggered and finally just from acute stress to the trees.

"Now as I said, there were some positive responders, so the real issue now becomes how much, which species, which site types, how much there are of those out on the landscape and where are they. So that is what we are trying to figure out right now. And so in those places, the effects of warming would be positive. It is simply those productive species aren't on those sites right now.

"The bottom line, to encapsulate the whole thing, it appears that based on what we know in these scenario projections, that climate warming of that magnitude would be a major, major disruption of the entire boreal forest system, and that disruption would amount to large scale mortality of some of our more productive forests and the necessity for some tree migration and movement of trees into areas where they are currently poorly productive, and a lot of challenges in getting all of that to happen in a fairly short amount of time.

"A little over 4 million acres have been affected by the spruce bark beetle. The larger or overstory trees that form the main forest canopy have been subjected to mortality. That means that generally, the guys in the plane looking down on the ground can map the area as showing mortality from the spruce bark beetle infestation. That threshold before they can identify it from a plane is about twenty percent. When 20 percent of the overstory trees are dead from the spruce bark beetle they generally are able to recognize it from the aerial survey and say yeah, the trees down there are killed by bark beetles. And in this outbreak the level of mortality has gone from this lower threshold of 20 percent all the way to 100 percent.

"This outbreak is so severe that a very substantial fraction of the area that has been affected, more than 4 million acres, has 100 percent overstory mortality. Generally trees that are four inches in diameter or smaller are not killed. In those places, it may be simply that the overstory dies, then the understory starts to mature.

However in a lot of places, and a substantial portion of the area, there is not the understory of the spruce, and the spruce has died over such a huge extent that the seeds cannot glide from surviving trees far enough to reach some of these depopulated localities. Spruce cover has been eliminated from substantial areas.

"We don't really know what is going to happen on a lot of those sites. We don't know if there will be a colonization of spruce that will grow back and if they do, when they exceed the four-inch threshold and start to get bigger, will they get hammered too from the spruce bark beetle? As near as we can tell, these outbreaks track these warm temperature episodes. So the outlook is not too favorable for spruce persistence in localities in southcentral Alaska, around Kenai, Anchorage and the copper river valley.

"I just looked at some data and tree cores that have been taken down there that have been sent to me from many sites. What we can say is many of the overstory trees are in the 170-270 year-old range. So it is pretty clear that nothing on this scale or intensity has happened in at least a century and probably 300 years and based upon what we know of climate variability, if you go back 300 years from the present, you go back to the little ice age, so you have to go back a thousand years before you reach a point where climatically it was likely that anything of this scale has happened in the past.

"We can conclude from that tentatively with the best evidence that we have that this is an extremely powerful event that has happened, and if the climate doesn't turn back cooler, it probably represents a semi-permanent change in the landscape by reducing the abundance and age structure of the spruce forest. And as to what will replace it, if any trees, we don't know and it does not look possible in places that there will be a good chance for long-persisting non-forest conditions where there used to be fairly productive spruce forest.

"Anything that is dependent upon the older spruce succession stages is going to be hugely reduced in abundance. And these include the larger-year-round resident woodpeckers, the black back and the northern three-toed. All the insect and lichen, all the organisms that are specialists in the older forest as well as organisms that may use older or mature forest cover for a certain type of year such as bears, or even moose need cover. To the degree it is not available to them, they will likely experience some population reduction.

"There may be some trumping factors. Especially if there are widespread fires that could be a big increase in moose numbers. But already we know moose population density is so great on the Kenai Peninsula that they prevent the Kenai Peninsula birch from successfully growing up into trees in a lot of places. So with the spruce eliminated horribly, you would expect it would shift toward birch, but that may not be possible with the moose populations that are there. And that may be why we get stuck in this non-forest semi-permanent condition.

"It is a big shift in everything. The large woody debris and the logs that represent the eventual fate of all of the large trees down there end up in stream channels. They are extremely important as an aquatic habitat factor and so there is going to be a big influx of that material over a period of time, and then it is going to be cut off because no matter what happens from now on, there is going to be a huge age class imbalance in the forest. A few decades down the road we are going to see some aquatic habitat impacts of this, with a big reduction of the input of new dead log material. It is just a complete chain of events that have been set off. It is not going to be a short-term effect. We are talking about landscape transformation for very long periods of time even if we make the assumption that everything would go back to normal tomorrow, which does not seem likely.

"It just so happens that most of the forest tree species, especially in the boreal forest region are simultaneously experiencing huge levels of outbreaks of insects that cause tree mortality. The best example would be the Larch. We estimate that most of the mature or larger larch in Alaska died in the beginning of the mid 1990s. They are dead now and we have relatively few larger or older larch surviving.

"That was the larch saw fly. Again it is the classic sort of insect. It's a moth that goes through these big outbreak numbers when there are warm conditions. This happened and persisted for a number of years. This assisted the insects in building up their population numbers. Then they just exploded across the landscape at huge population densities, found most of the mature larch and ate it up. In the first year of defoliation, heartier larch will survive.

The next year they will grow out sometimes even more because the insects actually convert plant material that otherwise might accumulate in hard to decompose compounds, they turn it into nitrogen-rich droppings from the insects on the forest floor. You can get a small decline or a small increase in production growth on the site that first year. But the second year of defoliation in a row, then it weakens the health of trees and it is starting to kill the weak trees. Then the third year, most of the trees if they are defoliated a third year in a row, then most of the trees die.

"That is exactly what happened. The outbreak was so severe, and so widespread, that most of the older larch died. And I could go on with other examples. The point is that associated with this unusually warm last couple of decades of the 20th century that we have had exactly what you would expect which is major outbreaks of the insects that affect trees and their outbreaks have been so severe and so persistent that they have caused unusually high levels of tree mortality to the point where we are talking about landscape changes.

"Their predictions are that the landscape outbreaks of spruce bark beetle probably have a limited potential to spread. The reason seems to be that when you go out to the coast, the spruce is a hybrid between sitka and white spruce. That is where most of the mortality is taking place. When you get into the sitka spruce stands, that is much more resistant to the insects. Sitka spruce can be killed by outbreaks of spruce bark beetle but much, much rarer, and usually they have to be severely injured by something that sets them up for it.

"As you go northward into the pure white spruce, it looks as if the cooler temperatures and the drier humidity limits the ability of the spruce bark beetles to build up in sufficient numbers so that there is probably a natural limit to the landscape level outbreaks to the north. It was just in this transition zone that they were uniquely vulnerable and the bugs just cleaned them out in that area.

"But there is another aspect to this. In addition to the already established insects that are usually under the control of colder temperatures, and now with the warmer temperatures have gone into these extreme outbreak levels, the warmer temperatures may be allowing insects that did not occur here before, and only south of here to become established. And we may have an example of that with the spruce bud worm. Rather than a beetle, it's a moth and instead of eating the bark, it tunnels into the new buds that are emerging.

"It is well known and well described through the southern boreal region of Canada. It is a major factor in boreal forests there. In general there is this temperature control that seems to help calm these big outbreaks, or limit it to background levels when it is cooler. The entomologists in Alaska didn't report it as an outbreak level in the boreal region here north of the Alaska Range before. And in the early 90s it first appeared in outbreak levels during a period of some of our warmest years. And it stayed around and appears now to be building up to new outbreak levels.

"In other words, it looks like it successfully established itself and now as we go through this warm-cool-warm-cool cycle, it's all being moved up a step so this newly established insect that can cause tree mortality has been established here. So that is another way in which the warmer temperatures are changing the forest. There are many places with tens of thousands of contiguous acres of every overstory tree dead. It is a very impressive site."

Fairbanks Climatologist Uma Bhatt said, "I drove south of Anchorage sometime in July and you just see huge stands of dead trees. It is pretty dramatic. I've seen photographs from researchers from the air. It is pretty amazing. I was in Tennessee before I moved here and there was another beetle there that ate through the pine trees so there were acres and acres of pine that were dead. Those were all planted by humans (in Tennessee). In Tennessee there is a wide variety of trees that can grow. In Alaska there are very few trees that can grow. There isn't a lot of variety. So when one gets killed or when one gets sick it is very easy for it to spread to other trees of the same species."

Molnia said, "Flying around Alaska, you see areas that were live, green needles that are now dead with brown needles. There is a major change."

Williams warned that "it is hard to imagine what (the dead forest) will be replaced by, because they originally thought it might be replaced by aspen or birch, but when you see that they are being attacked by leaf minors, with leaves that are just chewed up because of leaf minors that are prospering because of global warming, you wonder what will succeed them. It is unbelievable to understand that in such a short period of time that we have had this devastation, and much of it was not anticipated.

"That is the other story about disease vectors. Again you can say 'yeah, glaciers melt, sea levels rise, whatever' but there are I think so many diseases that we can't even anticipate as global warming advances."

Williams has a cabin near Anchorage overlooking Matangska Valley and Glacier. "Most of our old spruce on our property has died from spruce bark beetle. We tried to make the best of it by building our cabin with dead spruce. But, to look out and see basically every mature spruce die in the course of about five years was gut wrenching. We also have quaking aspen. Last summer for the first time we found leaf minors in our quaking aspen. So our quaking aspen instead of having brilliant green leaves in the summer and beautiful yellow leaves in the fall, last summers' leaves were gray, gray. And in the fall they were brown as the leaf minor chewed up the leaves.

"Last year is the first year that we had it. Fairbanks had it a couple years before but it is coming south in Alaska. And to think all of this in our lifetime."

CHAPTER 21

Vanishing Tundra

With increasing temperatures and precipitation, the tree line continues to move north, within a few dozen miles of the Arctic Ocean. This encroaching change means the elimination of the tundra, and questions the survival of the animals that depend upon that fertile wetland ecosystem.

The Greenpeace report "Vanishing Ice" describes the importance of the coastal plain. "Birds migrate here from six continents to nest on coastal tundra. Millions of seabirds raise their young in colonies along the water's edge. Streams and coastal spawning grounds contribute to the rich fisheries of this region. Caribou wander the tundra, also home to wolves, fox and a variety of small mammals. These living resources are likewise vital to the survival of coastal people."

A World Fund for Nature report of April 2000 warns climate change could eliminate 50 percent of rare Arctic bird populations. The report states that higher temperatures will cause wooded forests to advance northward, replacing the Arctic tundra, an essential breeding area for millions of birds. The report finds that the Arctic water birds most threatened by the global warming include the critically-endangered red-breasted goose, tundra bean goose, spoonbilled sandpiper and emperor goose.

With a global temperature increase of only 1.7 degrees by 2070, all of these birds would lose more than 50 percent of their habitat, the report notes. More than two-thirds of all geese and nearly 95 percent of all calidrid waders breed in the Arctic. The study forecasts that a 40 percent to 57 percent loss of tundra in the next 100 years may decrease habitat for 5 million geese and 7.5 million calidrid waders.

"This study once more underlines the urgent need to reduce the emissions of global warming gases to slow the rate of climate change," the researchers write. "In order to facilitate adaptation to a changed climate, we need to seriously consider changes in habitat management."

The vanishing tundra means a loss of habitat for all tundra species. As the forest marches north, as Glen Juday warns, this could mean a loss of open tundra habitat for migrating birds, musk ox, caribou, and more, said retired Arctic National Wildlife Refuge biologist Fran Mauer.

"Many of those (bird) species are adapted to open tundra environments. They don't nest in forests. You don't find tundra-nesting birds nesting in the forest already. So when we wonder if they would do so if there were no other place, you see the problem is that this isn't going to happen in one year's time. The forests aren't going to pop up on the north slope in one year such that these tundra nesting birds would fly up there next year and find a forest there and have no place else to go.

"It would happen more gradually and populations would make adjustments accordingly with the gradual movement of forests northward. With tundra habitat shrinking you can only support so many birds per unit area and eventually those bird populations would probably shrink. So in the long run, some species that require tundra habitat may either have to adapt or disappear or go somewhere else. If there is still tundra somewhere else, like the Canadian Arctic islands, some of those species might persist in those areas. But the total populations would be less than they are now just because of the shrunken amount of habitat available. It is just very hard to get into specifics about this stuff because we've never lived through it before.

"I don't know of any significant musk ox populations living and surviving in forest country. We do see them in tree-line settings sometimes, both in northcentral Canada and we've had some musk ox come across the south side of the Brooks Range where there are sparse forest communities. But I don't know of any thriving musk ox populations in continuous forest lands.

More forest would probably shrink habitat for musk ox as well. Tundra or grassland open country is what they seem to need and are evolved for. Living in forests probably wouldn't work for them."

The authors raft on the Hulahula River as it enters the coastal plain in the Arctic National Wildlife Refuge during his expedition in 1991.

CHAPTER 22

Change in Snowfall

With some aspects of weather, like temperature, glaciers, permafrost and pack ice, it is clear that the overall trend is strikingly in one direction. With other impacts of climate change, it is a change from traditional patterns that is different. This is the case with snowfall, where in some places and times it is less, whereas other times it is greater. Though this change is not uniform, it is having major negative effects throughout Alaska.

"There used to be heavy snowfall in the spring time; there used to be three feet of snow where we walked and now I don't see it anymore. Instead of dog mushing, we have dog slushing," said Jimmie Toolie, Savoonga's eldest elder in a Greenpeace report.

"It's been pretty mild the last few years. We even had rain in January. Last year, we hardly had snow on the ground. Spring was a month early. This year almost the same thing but we had a little more snow than last year," said Benjamin Neakok.

"It's freezing up later and breaking up a lot sooner," said Benjamin Pungawiyi of Savoonga. "We didn't have much snow this year. When we go to our camp we have to cross these mountains. People had to pack up right away and come home because the trail conditions were really deteriorating because of a lack of snow and more bare rocks.

"As far as freezing up, we hardly got any snow until November. Usually we have our first snowfall around the end of September. During the summer months we have clouds and rain and drizzle. Now there's hardly any clouds or rain or drizzle. There's more sunshine. It's a lot warmer than before."

James said, "The last two years, we got too much snow because of the climate change. Due to that the caribou did not get to the core calving ground. They calved short and that killed a lot of calves. Sometimes, because of climate change we don't get enough snow. Snow works like insulation. Then the ground freezes deeper and the fish die. The hibernating animals die, the grizzly, muskrat, ground squirrel, mouse and beaver. It's too cold. They get cold too. If there is not enough snow, their dens get colder."

Pam Miller of Arctic Connections said, "The biggest impacts that I have personally seen are the change in the chronology of the spring season, where snow melt happens earlier and caribou calving is about a week earlier than it was a couple decades ago. And there is somewhat earlier nesting of birds and things like the ducks.

"Global warming is climate change, so there are a lot of unusual situations, where for example in a couple years, the Porcupine Caribou Herd calved way south in Canada. And that is highly unusual because of the way the snow pack is. It affects them on their whole migration route, the timing of the animals on the Arctic coastal plain. As someone who travels to that area, you do see that kind of impact.

"Living in Alaska, you hear it is getting warmer. Our winters are getting warmer. And it's true and some people appreciate that but the last two winters we had almost no snow, because the climate patterns are different. There was no ice skating until February or March, and no skiing until March.

"That's a personal effect. This year we have tons of snow. But the patterns seem to be more unpredictable and it is a very real thing. It is not just people who are on a day-to-day basis working on environmental issues, but people who are living out on the land. They see it. The tree line is moving northward in the Arctic Refuge for example."

Edith Float from Mekoryuk said, "I noticed changes in the snow. That was maybe 20 years ago, but lately the snow has come late. When I was young, the snow would come in late September. And now the snow is mostly rain."

CHAPTER 23

Interference with Arctic Oil Exploration

One of the most dramatic impacts of climate change has been the shortening of the season in which the oil industry is allowed to explore and develop for oil. In order to protect the fragile tundra, federal and state regulators required the oil industry to only develop when the ground was frozen 12 inches deep and had 6 inches of snow cover.

While in 1970 more than 200 days met the above criteria, with climate change, only 103 days met the criteria in 2002. Cox News Service reported in 2003, "global warming, which most climate experts blame mainly on large-scale burning of fossil fuels, is interfering with efforts in Alaska to discover yet more oil."

But instead of realizing the significance of this change as a global need to reduce greenhouse gases, and invest in the proven solar and wind alternative instead of more fossil fuels, the state of Alaska has instead changed the rules, to allow more damage to the tundra by further opening the season of oil devastation to the fragile north slope by up to 6 weeks.

Initially, the study of tundra impacts was to "refine our understanding of the tundra's disturbances," But when the study was released in December, 2004, the state said it needed to change the standards to open the season longer because it is "a problem for Alaskans who rely on the oil industry: in other words, for all of us. We need to lengthen the season." The December 3, 2004 press release by the state of Alaska admitted that the change in seasons was caused by "warming weather."

Environmental groups charge that the existing standards

were not protecting the tundra, and the changes will only increase already unacceptable levels of damage. One of the lead environmentalists working on this issue happens to be a college friend of mine. Kelly Hill Scanlon and I were in the Ohio University Ecology Club, which succeeded in getting recycling institutionalized at our university and protecting lands around Athens back in the late 80s and early 90s. Now she is the Arctic Campaigner for the Northern Alaska Environmental Center in Fairbanks, Alaska. She is also monitoring the test sites that the state is using to make new standards for oil development.

I stayed with Hill-Scanlon, her husband, a fisheries biologist with the state, and their three-month-old daughter during my visit to Fairbanks in late August, 2004. Hill-Scanlon explained why the state of Alaska is so predisposed to wanting oil development. "The state of Alaska in the constitution says lands for the benefit of the citizens of the state—that's meant mine it, drill it, log it. The state of Alaska owns all subsurface rights even for federal lands. That is why the state is so money hungry for the drilling of federal lands.

"That's something we're trying to combat. The benefit does not have to mean economic gain—the caribou are a benefit. You can't put a dollar value on it. It's all these foreign companies coming into our state and taking our resources. Is that really benefiting our state? It's disrupting the caribou in the NPRA.

"The work season used to go from November through early April. Over the last 5 years, that window has declined because of global warming to where sometimes January is the first date to travel. That does not work for the oil companies. They need to build ice roads first. The Department of Energy gave a grant to do a study by the Department of Natural Resources. In the proposal it says 'due to global warming'—the oil companies agree that global warming is real because they have signed on.

"They have a plot 3 miles outside of Deadhorse and one in Happy Valley." Kelly witnessed the plots with the NAEC. "They have 30 plots of land 50 meters long. In July, 2003, the

DNR got baseline data from the plots—the vegetation, the species, the soil, the moisture level, heights of plants.

"There were testing dates in September, October, November, December and January. They tested 5 vehicles and left some untouched. They would do a figure 8. That was this past winter (2003-2004). DNR went back up this summer and re-measured everything.

"A bulldozer in October ripped up the ground. It's not only a year since the damage. Tundra damage often does not show for more than a year. One problem is there is just one year of study. They are trying to get Yale to pick it up. The governor wanted the results released in September. It is basically a rush job. DNR said not by September but by November. Scientifically there is a problem. There is no peer review.

"They're going to do peer review, after it is released. That's like letting the fox in the henhouse and then trying to get it out. We know the political motivation is to open the tundra earlier. The scientists can only extrapolate it to those plots, not to all the areas of the north slope.

"We think the feds will probably adopt the findings of the study. I went there last summer. From the October tests, there was significant damage. The bulldozer track was like mud. We want to make sure it is sound science, peer reviewed and we want to make sure it will really protect the tundra and not just buy a few more days for the oil companies.

"We've hired Bruce Forbes, an international tundra expert. He's doing an independent analysis of the study. He found the methodology is fine but the results are not. That's how you do the thing politically, not scientifically. The Governor (Frank Murkowski) wanted it earlier because I think he thought it would have benefited his run.

Forbes found that the tundra will continue to show damage from vehicle disturbance for two years after the impact. Thus, by only studying the impacts a few months after the vehicles drive through, they are missing the long-term effects. Hill-

Scanlon said that they failed to employ the proper experts, and the report was based on politics, not science. Forbes concurred, with questions as to the expertise of the scientists, and a volley of criticisms with a study that has far more to do with politics and the interests of the oil industry and very little science.

Guntner Weller said climate change is impacting infrastructure, roads and pipelines. "There are huge problems when the permafrost melts, and industrial facilities collapse. For example with the Trans Alaskan Pipeline, we've talked to the engineers. About half of the pipeline is buried, the other half is above ground supported by a steel frame. The steel frame is artificially kept frozen through a refrigerant, so the base of the steel structures are embedded in permafrost. As it gets warmer, the permafrost table goes down, the support begins to sink and they have to be re-engineered, and drilled deeper. These are impacts that are not insurmountable, but they cost more money. There is an economic impact."

Williams also noted impacts on oil and gas development. "The other infrastructure story is how climate change is reducing the period in which oil companies can develop oil and gas using ice on the North Slope. The number of days has been reduced drastically. The state of Alaska documented this well. So for years and years the oil industry has relied on ice roads, ice pads and ice technology to do relatively low cost, low impact exploration on the North Slope. Now the season is becoming so short, that it is no longer becoming economic in some instances for the oil industry to do ice-based oil exploration and development. So they are looking at other technologies with rigor.

"Andy Revkin with the *New York Times* was up here recently, and he is doing an article on the new technology, the large wheeled machines. The state of Alaska is trying to determine how much ice and snow is necessary to do oil development. They are trying to redefine that down so they have a longer season. That is a bit of an ironic impact of global warming because the primary cause of global warming, oil and gas development is now being impacted by it, and now the industry is trying to come up with exceptions to deal with that."

Wohlforth said, "The oil industry has noticed the same things. They are only allowed to do operations during time periods when the ground is frozen hard, and that is becoming a shorter and shorter time period. They are actually running into problems because they do not have enough time period of hard frozen ground, which is kind of ironic. They are the ones producing the fossil fuels, and the impacts of the fossil fuels appears to be making the ground thaw so that they cannot do their job."

Pam Miller of Arctic Connections said that the oil and gas industry already cannot do its activities without damaging the tundra, so making it less stringent will only further increase the damage that is already at unacceptable levels. She warned of more alarming impacts as toxic waste dumps that were frozen into the permafrost, and considered contained, are now melting and being released into the surrounding environment. Miller noted that the Alaska Department of Environmental Conservation has done work at well sites around Prudhoe Bay at existing oil fields.

"What they find is around the well, where it goes down into the ground the permafrost is melted. And you typically have a pretty contaminated site there. They consider in the Prudhoe field every one of those is a contaminated site. So when you get to the point when ultimately the oil runs out and they are no longer connected and they are not going to pump any more from the ground, you are going to have lots of those sorts of sites.

"Another thing, there are situations where in the past the military buried a lot of toxic and radioactive waste in the Arctic. In the National Petroleum Reserve Area (NPRA) in northwest Alaska there are a lot of old waste dumps and there are also military sites where they had landfills off Kaktovik in Barter Island and they are eroding into the ocean now. The sites that may have been 'sealed into the permafrost,' are now melting and leaching out. There are a couple places where they've closed out a lot of the drilling waste pits and dug a huge big hole and thought they could secure that material in a site that would be frozen, and it actually didn't work like that. And to presume that a site that now may be frozen into the ground, that is not a safe assumption for a way out.

"The oil industries own operations are now coming back to bite them. Because of the global warming, their ability to rely on ice roads to access either development sites that might be built without a road, there are a couple of those already, or for their new exploration programs, they are realizing that they don't have the working season that they used to. And you can find that citation from the Department of Natural Resources report on the shortening seasons.

"But what they are wanting to do is very political, in my opinion. Basically the assumptions of the DNR study going into it is that if they measure the snow and hardness in the ground in a different way, or if they use a different standard, that they will still be able to protect the tundra and basically this will allow tundra travel earlier in the fall.

"There are a couple of problems with what they are doing. One is they are only going to have a couple study sites. They are only going to look at disturbance next summer. That is it, not the long-term damage to the tundra. They are not setting up what criteria for change is acceptable, and having that peer reviewed. And how much damage is a problem? On the state land with the state's priority of land use, they might be willing to trash a lot more tundra.

"But I would not say that the tundra travel criteria was necessarily working to begin with, especially as they go into new areas. The 6 inches of snow and 12 inches of frost standard, they didn't measure it throughout the areas where industry would travel anyway. There's a lot of variability with the terrain, the nature of the snow cover. Basically in recent years they divided up the portion between the Canning and the Colville into quadrants, and they refined it a little bit in looking at how much snow and frost there was there. Most of the samples were taken right by Prudhoe Bay, right by the airfield, where it was easy to access. But it did not take into account how the different vegetation may be exposed, or even things like open water in the streams, and how soon you can build an ice bridge across the Colville River or across the other rivers if they are freezing later. It is not going to capture that obstacle to building an ice road. And finally, those studies that were done on seismic testing in the Arctic Refuge showed that pretty much across the board, you need at least 8 or 10 inches of snow in order to prevent damage.

"The old standard may not have been precautionary enough. And I quite frankly think that they'll figure out a way no matter what the results say to get out there earlier in the state lands. And the NPRA, which is a vast area now under threat, they had a stipulation for the four million acres that were available for leasing right next to the Colville River in the northeast corner of that area. And when they did the northwest area, they changed that standard and they made it really wimpy and said 'you have to protect the ground.'

"They've already done away with the standard even though the state standard that was funded by the Department of Energy is not even done. So clearly industry wants its way, and is getting it politically in the NPRA and on the state lands you know they are getting some more information. I think better scientific basis for what they are doing is helpful. It is not going to solve the problem that there is not a long season for them to build ice roads.

"With the existing standards, there is still damage from off road vehicles, seismic exploration, cat trains, fort camps that they haul around. From repeated laying down ice roads, from repeated use of land from the rollagon trails, there are scars across the state land even with that state standard. So it's hard to say how much worse it will be. I think there are a lot of unknowns, especially if they are moving into new areas that they haven't operated in before that are hillier, that may have more tussocks (knobs of vegetation) that may have different permafrost composition such as up near the inland foothills of the state land and the NPRA."

The National Academy of Sciences Cumulative Environmental Impact study of human effects on the north slope of Alaska reports that, "because the climate is expected to warm so rapidly that the effects of current activities could be much greater on the permafrost landscape than would be the case if the climate were relatively stable." The academy of sciences report continues, "The largest human contribution to climate warming is the burning of fossil fuel hydrocarbon fuels. ...The resultant climate change affects the North Slope probably more than lower latitude areas.... It is an important factor that must be considered."

Miller said, "There has never been enough water to build ice roads in the Arctic Refuge to begin with. The fact that ice roads aren't feasible from the industry perspective because the season is so short, it could exacerbate the limitations there certainly, but there was already a problem. There is already a problem with Alaskan snow cover. You can find a six-inch average in the Arctic Refuge most winters, but it didn't protect the tundra when they implemented that standard."

As far as a solution to climate change, Miller said, "I think really you are talking about the bigger energy policy issue, and are we going to take a far-sighted view to change towards a new future sustainable energy policy that can reduce our fossil fuel emissions that are contributing to global warming. And from that standpoint, it doesn't make sense to sacrifice a unique resource like the Arctic Refuge, when your broader policy needs to make the shift from the oil age of fossil fuel development to what is needed now." Miller said the investment that is needed now is in renewables and conservation to get clean energy faster with the goal of reducing fossil fuel emissions.

CHAPTER 24

Dire Future

W ith climate change expected to increase as more greenhouse gases are emitted each year, the future of the Arctic and Alaska looks bleak, with more dying forests, shrinking glaciers, retreating pack ice and crumbling shorelines. Fran Mauer called the impacts of climate change in the Arctic "unprecedented in the history of the planet."

With the Testimonies Project, Ritzman said Greenpeace "wanted to work to educate Americans on Global Warming and raise the level of concern. The second component was we wanted to do something directly to combat climate change. Greenpeace was unique in that it is international, and they did the science to prove that we are getting to the critical point of no return. We cannot burn a quarter of our known reserves. So there is no point in finding new reserves. We should use that effort to find renewable energy sources."

Williams warned that many of the effects of climate change cannot be mitigated. "Some of (climate change's impacts) can be mitigated. Oh well, you can move villages. You can rebuild highways. There is certain mitigation that you can do. But other things can't be mitigated. If polar bears become extinct because of global warming, if native cultures become extinct because of global warming, these impacts can't be mitigated. And I think that is a very important point to make. Because global warming is more palatable if you think, 'Oh we'll just throw enough money in mitigation.' We'll just deal with it as the impacts become known.

"But, if we go into global warming with the knowledge that there is a likelihood if not the inevitability of profound impacts that cannot be mitigated, I think it changes the way we look at our responsibility to address global warming now. The other question with mitigation to, is if we talk about moving villages at $100 million a pop here, $100 million a pop there, and all of the other costs associated with global warming, the impacts on fisheries, the impacts on Agriculture, wildlife and disease, and start adding up those costs, pretty soon I think that we as a society can conclude that the costs of prevention are a lot less than the costs of global warming. I really do believe that Alaska helps demonstrate both the extent of the costs that you can mitigate, but also the extent of the costs you cannot mitigate. And that is one of Alaska's greatest lessons is that global warming is profoundly costly."

Juday warned that all the predictions of climate change's future impacts would lead to a massive loss of forests in Alaska, far more than has already been seen.

"All of the scenarios basically raise the temperatures to levels where we would begin to see by the end of the century the temperature threshold at which the trees would not be able to grow on certain sites. So here is what I project. We would see continuing levels of very large-scale outbreaks of insects that kill trees.

"That has always happened, there has always been some of that around. But we are going to see a larger percent of our landscape is going to be made up of big patches of dead trees under conditions like the scenarios produced.

"Number two, there would very likely then be a lot of fires, because those sites would probably burn. And the forests, once they got going would be burning lower moisture content fuels so they would burn more sites and burn more thoroughly. So basically we would have larger and more frequent forest disturbance from insects and from fires. So we would have fewer older forests in any given time and more younger forest. And as we got near the end of the scenario time we would see forests unable to regenerate in certain landscape types so natural grasslands would become a more important part of the landscape." He predicted large prairies where once there were forests.

"You would see permafrost thawing. Fifty to fifty-five percent of the boreal forest is made up of black forest dominated stands. Almost all of that is under-laid with permafrost. You would start to see a substantial amount of that permafrost start to thaw. You would see big sink holes and low spots that would begin to collect water around the trees and you would see a lot of that in these low elevation black spruce permafrost types, and then eventually some of it would drain out, some of it would remain ponded wetlands, permanent wetlands. You would generally see a drying out of the landscape and then you would see as well forests moving up in elevation and possibly getting north of the Brooks Range barrier and getting to establish on favorable sites in the North Slope tundra.

"The scenarios produced climates that would allow white spruce to grow in the tundra foothills region of the North Slope." The chance of seeds getting there would be unpredictable, he said, so the actual trees may take longer to appear, but they would be able to grow there under the new climate models.

"Researchers in Siberia have recovered some frozen tree remains from the permafrost," Juday continued. "From 8,000 to 6,000 years ago, there were trees all the way to the coast of the Arctic Ocean in Siberia. The summers were warmer during that period of time, and over a period of thousands of years, the trees gradually retreated. It happened in major cooling episodes.

"If the scenarios of warming are correct, it is very reasonable to project that trees will make it all the way to the Arctic coast, but it probably would not be the full canopy. It would likely be a forest tundra, with trees in more favorable sites, interspersed with tundra in between. The tundra would likely change with fewer tussocks. The shrubs would get a lot taller. It would produce some things helpful to caribou survival, some things negative, but most tundra animals would see a squeeze on their populations."

"It is a pretty straightforward proposition. You don't have

to believe in a doubling of earth's population," Juday said. "If we humans continue to pump out greenhouse gas emissions, if we just continue what we are doing now, we will build up a significant problem for the survival of elements of biodiversity. We either come to some limitation or slow the rates or reverse the increases or we will have to deal with those things.

"The only debate really is how long. Now, could humans survive on an earth with a severely greenhouse effect-impacted climate, well probably yes, but there would be major effects.

"We have to recognize that a significant advance of the forest into the tundra would amplify the climate warming. With spruce forests, 80-90 percent of the energy is absorbed, whereas snow-covered tundra reflects 80-90 percent. Converting smooth, dry snow-covered tundra to rough, dark spruce covered forest would produce more warming."

Compounding the problem more, Juday said "the amount of carbon stored in the boreal forests and forest soils is very large. The amount that could be converted to methane or CO_2 is a substantial fraction of what is already in the atmosphere. This would amplify the warming. So it looks like already one of the things that land managers in boreal regions need to look at is ways to sequester carbon dioxide."

Josefino Comiso also warned of accelerating impacts of climate change. "Modeling studies confirm that if you have so much increase in carbon dioxide in the atmosphere, you have an increase of temperature as well on account of the greenhouse effect and also the feedbacks. You get the ice retreating for example, you get more solar energy to the surface of the Earth and this furthers warming."

"We really have to be serious about this impact. Because even though we are sure now about the large variability in the perennial ice cover in the Arctic, the trend is very significant toward a reduction of ice. When we deal with the planet, we need to be very careful with the activities of human beings, and make sure that we are not the cause of a permanent harm on this planet, which is the only planet that we know of that has intelligent life in the universe. We don't want to take the risk of losing that because we were negligent for doing what is right for our system."

Juday said, "The message to other folks in other parts of the world who are at risk is get ready. Because when it happens, you've got to adjust. There are people who do have plans for using other landscapes and resources, and they won't have the luxuries that we do in Alaska. You know oh, that park is going to be less tundra a little more forest and the lower elevations will be a little less forest and a little more grasslands. We are not going to be all that upset about that and we will track the wildlife and you know maybe there will be a few things that we need to do.

"But in other parts of the world, you won't have that luxury. You'd better get ready. I think you've seen in the last several years in the West extensive fires have occurred more frequently over a greater area with a greater severity and people had been planning on using those trees for various things. They put their homes in those various places. And nature hasn't been too kind to those expectations that you had. So be prepared."

Researcher Phil Jones of the University of East Anglia found that analysis of tree rings, ice cores, corals and historical records indicate that the 1990s were the warmest decade of the millennium. He also found that seven of the world's ten warmest years occurred in the 1990s.

What makes the situation so dire is the entrenched commitment of anti-environmental lobbying and policies of coal, oil, auto and airline industries and lawmakers (mostly Republican) that are blocking efforts like the Kyoto Protocol that would begin to make some real cuts in global warming gas emissions. Syndicate columnist Molly Ivins wrote, "The response of Alaska's Republican right (to climate change) is to slash and burn, subsidize mining and give tax breaks to oil and gas companies for exploration. Cronyism and favors for special-interest groups have become the hallmarks of state government. Gov. Frank Murkowski even appointed his own daughter to the U.S. Senate, a staggering example of nepotism."

Comiso warned that, "one of my concerns is if you don't do something, there is always the possibility of abrupt climate change, and there is evidence from the paleo record that this has occurred. Something like that could be catastrophic for humans. Therefore I value doing something about it."

Alaskans "are the canary in the mine shaft," Weller said, imploring people to take notice of climate change and begin to make the needed changes in government, industry and personal activities to reduce greenhouse gas emissions.

CHAPTER 25

Human-Caused
or Natural?

While many people agree that there are major changes in the weather, not everyone understands the solid scientific proof that human burning of fossil fuels is the primary cause of the climate change.

Uma Bhatt said, "The other night I was sitting at an American Meteorological Society meeting in Seattle with a bunch of scientists, and one of them said 'you know 15 years ago if you asked the average scientist if you see a human impact, 50 percent of the people would have said yes.' But now if you asked I would say most atmospheric scientists, probably 95 percent would say yes, because in the last 15 years there have been a lot of pieces of evidence that have come in. It is not just looking at one time sequence, it is looking at all of the things that come in. And for me one of the most compelling pieces of evidence is if you look at nighttime temperatures. Because then that is a radiational impact. You see a strong significant trend in nighttime temperatures globally. That is where you really see it. So I would be very comfortable in saying that we do see human impacts on the climate."

Josefino Comiso said scientists are convinced that human greenhouse gas pollution is to blame for the unusual weather. "We are now in a position I think where we can construct models a lot more accurately than 10-20 years ago. We have a much better understanding of physics than before. We have much better satellite data than before, not just in resolution but in quality. We have much more comprehensive data sets. The data that climatologists could only dream of 20 years ago is now available.

"We can say with a lot more confidence in terms of the impact of carbon dioxide and other greenhouse gases. It's indeed a big impact. Even if you consider the large variability and the Arctic Oscillations, we show a much greater association of greenhouse gases with the warming."

Guntner Weller said, "I am also totally convinced that anthropogenic is a significant change in climate change and this is the consensus of most scientists from around the world. More recently, since the global climate change has been more known, I have looked at the impacts of climate change. It is up to us to also say what the potential impacts on climate change are."

In reply to those who deny climate change or its negative affects, Patricia Cochran, executive director of the Alaska Native Science Commission said, "They obviously don't live in the Arctic."

Former Boston Globe reporter and editor Ross Gelbspan wrote a book in 1997, "The Heat is On" about the fossil fuel industry efforts to discredit climate change. He found that the conclusion that human-caused greenhouse gas emissions are causing the planet to warm up are the result of the "most rigorously peer-reviewed scientific collaboration in history. The contradictory statements of a tiny handful of discredited scientists, funded by big coal and big oil, represent a deliberate—and extremely reckless—campaign of deception and disinformation."

On March 1, 1999, the American Geophysical Union issued a strong position statement on climate change. The group, representing 35,000 Earth and planetary scientists, warned "there is no known geologic precedent for the transfer of carbon from the Earth's crust to the atmosphere" in the amounts comparable to fossil-fuel burning without simultaneous changes to the climate.

The atmospheric concentration of carbon dioxide has risen from 280 parts per million in 1800 to 380 parts per million today due to the combustion of fossil fuels. "What's happening to our environment is not natural. It's a problem of our own making," said Eileen Claussen, President of the Pew Center on Global Climate Change in a November, 2004 report. "The longer we delay in reducing greenhouse gas emissions, the greater the problem will become."

"Historically, the Earth has never been over 290 parts per million carbon dioxide," said Ohio State University Geological Science Professor Dr. Lonnie Thompson on National Public Radio, December 17, 2004. "We are engaging in a giant experiment, with disastrous and often unforeseen consequences. Humanity is adding 2 parts per million more carbon into the atmosphere every year," the scientist said.

Comiso said, "the question is to what extent the increases in greenhouse gases would cause a warming. And this has been attempted by several scientists around the world who have published their results. The question is the amount is not clear. They have reached the stage that now we are getting global data sets. We recently launched satellites that can measure parameters with greater precision.

"To understand the climate system, you have to have input numbers from different sources. But now, with the use of satellite data, we have greater interpretation of greater atmospheric parameters. So with this greater global data set, and with more powerful computers that allow us to run the model longer, taking 8,000 years of climate data over the last 8,000 years, used to take several weeks. It now takes several days.

"As we are getting able to get better and better models that are more able to represent the climate, then we are able to have better and better confidence about the real impact of fossil fuels burning on the climate. And then we are able to sort out what impact CO_2 and other sources of greenhouse gases are contributing to the warming that we are seeing right now.

"You have a lot of research going on in addition to the research that we have been doing around the Earth that looks at the confidence level for all of these studies. And it is hard to establish that we are one hundred percent confident mainly because we just do not have enough data. But we are moving very rapidly in that direction. It is very clear that the weight of data shows that we are on the right track. We know that the science is there.

"I don't think that there is any question right now that the Arctic is warming. Even people who are very much against the Kyoto Protocol for example accept the fact that global warming is occurring. Unfortunately, it is much more difficult to establish that global warming is one hundred percent caused by the burning of fossil fuels. But we have enough data to show the probabilities are quite high that CO_2 is the cause of much of the global warming. Recent modeling studies support the fact that the warming is caused by CO_2 and other greenhouse gas emissions. You can shoot down the models, and say that they are not perfect, but the statistics are there, and the magnitude and the rate have to be refined to reach the point where we are 99 percent sure."

While some may point to isolated areas of cooling, Comiso said satellite data can sort that out and show that on the whole, the trend is toward warming. "The global climate system is very complex. With global satellite data you see warming in some areas, and cooling in others. That is just the way the system works."

"You know that the direction is right," Comiso said of the proof that humans are warming the planet. "The magnitude might not be right, but the direction is right. You know that we understand the physics well enough to understand the direction well enough, and from the trends."

But coal and oil industries have unleashed a massive publicity campaign to discredit the reality of climate change. Fran Mauer said "a lot of the corporate interests that have a lot at stake have been actively involved in promoting confusion. The best analogy that sheds light on that phenomenon is to look at the tobacco industries' response to the growing number of studies showing the risks of smoking, and the campaigns that the tobacco industry engaged in. And some are still involved." He said on a broader scale fossil fuel and auto industry corporate interests are engaging in similar tactics with climate change.

Part Two

SOLUTIONS

CHAPTER 26

Taking the Heat Off: Slowing Climate Change

Science Writer William K. Stevens called global warming's impacts on Alaska an "ecological holocaust." Christian Science Monitor reporter Ed Hunt found this term fitting, because as in the Holocaust of World War II, so many tried to look the other way and ignore what was happening. Also, as in the earlier part of the second world war, Hunt proclaims, the world's great nations are preparing and uniting to fight, while the U.S. has yet to join in. "I have little doubt we will soon join the fight," Hunt writes. "We can't deny it any longer. Something is happening."

With four percent of the world's population, the United States produces 25 percent of the world's greenhouse gas emissions. Instead of following the guidelines of the Kyoto Protocol, and cutting emissions, the United States is greatly increasing its emissions. They are expected to rise 43 percent by the year 2020.

George Bush caused a major rift in global efforts to combat climate change by pledging upon his "election" that he would oppose the United States' ratification of the Kyoto Protocol. The Kyoto Protocol formed out of the first framework convention on climate change at the Earth Summit in Rio de Janeiro, Brazil. Its goal was to get beyond science and began an actual reduction of climate change gases. One of the many rifts that occurred in the global agreement was between developed and developing countries. Because it was largely developed countries that caused climate change, developing countries opposed efforts to include them in the forced reduction of greenhouse gases. Largely because of this disparity of requirements, that would force developed countries to begin cutting emissions first, the U.S. Senate initially resoundingly rejected the Kyoto Protocol. However, global awareness of the crisis prompted many senators to change to favor the needed treaty. Most of the rest of the world have nearly unanimously come to the conclusion that the small changes in the Kyoto Protocol are at least a basic need to shift us toward reducing emissions instead of greatly increasing them as we are now.

Even some of the staunchest conservatives are admitting there is a crisis. "This is a creeping disaster," Republican Alaskan Senator Ted Stevens said. "We're not even sure it's covered by existing (federal) disaster loans." Senator John McCain, chairman of the Senate Commerce Committee, said Stevens' description of the effects of climate change in Alaska are "an argument for doing more than increasing our (computer) modeling capabilities."

The climatologist said that "there is no question that global warming's impact on Alaska has received a tremendous amount of media attention. The whole story of Alaskan climate impacts has been extremely popular with the media. I can't count how many television crews have been here, including BBC, New Zealand, Arts and Entertainment channel, two weeks ago we had American Scientific Frontiers. We've had Alan Alda, the actor from M*A*S*H and lots of reporters. On average, I get one or two calls per week on this topic. There is an enormous interest in this.

"Thirty-five years ago there certainly was not the same amount of interest. But the greenhouse effect became popular 15-20 years ago. Before there were other concerns, the nuclear winter was a big topic in those days. That has completely faded. This more recent interest in climate change is a concern that we are screwing up the climate and what can we do about it."

Bush policies have not been favorable for finding a solution to climate change, Weller said. "The U.S. has said they are not interested. There is a new climate policy to develop policies. We can always do more science. But I think the evidence is in hand. It is time to do something about it. In the U.S. Congress and White House, they are trying to sideline it, but I see in other sectors much greater interest. In municipalities, this issue is taking a hell of a lot more interest than in DC. Big oil industries are taking interest. Unfortunately, most are European like BP and Shell. The insurance industry is clearly interested in understanding more and doing more.

Mauer said, "One thing that is interesting is it seems that some people in the insurance industry are starting to pay attention, because if weather patterns become more powerful and more erratic and more unpredictable, they might be forking out a heck of a lot more money for damages. Some of the big insurance folks started showing up at climate change conferences as much as ten years ago. So they are starting to wonder if something is going on, and they want to know about it so they can change their calculations on their insurance rates. They can be wiped out if things start changing more than they factor in."

Renewable Energy Expert Chris Rose said, "Some interesting developments on (the externality) front is that some of the biggest insurance companies in the world, such as Swiss Re, which is the second biggest insurance company in the world asks its insurers what they are doing about global warming. Because Swiss Re keeps paying out all of these huge costs for all these extreme weather events. It is the same thing with Munich Re, which is one of the largest re-insurance companies in the world. In the last 40-50 years, the amount of payouts because of extreme weather events has gone up 10 times."

Weller said, "In time I think the popular opinion will swing the politicians around. I think that as long as it doesn't cost too much, there is still the interest in getting an SUV to drive to the local supermarket. With efforts to put tighter fuel economies, we have a long way to go. I hope that reason will prevail because there is no other way.

"We are a pretty wasteful nation. I think in all levels of society things could be done to improve the situation. Internationally we should talk about Kyoto. On the economic side, I think there are measures that could easily try to achieve the targets of the Kyoto Protocol by fuel efficiency and recycling. I think it is nonsense that it would hurt the U.S. Economy. The Japanese are building fuel-efficient cars. The Dutch and Denmark are building wind generators. There are lots of things that we can do that make money.

"Down at the various levels, city planners are beginning to take it seriously, particularly in coastal areas. You can recycle, you can walk, you cannot use the elevator, you can drive a more efficient vehicle. I think there needs to be a moral commitment, and they can actually do something about it. I think the whole engagement of pollution as a moral issue is very important. We need to get the word out that this is something that we should take seriously, and perhaps in our own small way contribute to get people more involved.

Another indication about the seriousness of global warming is that even those who largely cause the problem, and therefore have been trying to discredit the sound science of climate change, are now admitting that it is indeed real.

Even the American Petroleum Institute said, "While consensus on climate change remains a work in progress, we do know enough to take the risk seriously and to rule out inaction as an option."

According to the Intergovernmental Panel on Climate Change, in order to stabilize greenhouse gases in the atmosphere, global emissions must be reduced to at least 60 percent below 1990 levels. That is a radical change in the way the world uses energy. This will require a new industrial revolution with a major decrease in fossil fuels and a blossoming of the already proven solar and wind energy technologies.

Comiso said that she thinks that policy makers should ratify the Kyoto Protocol. "I think there is enough evidence, and for me the most compelling evidence is there is so many pieces of evidence coming in."

Native peoples in Alaska have returned to using dog sleds instead of snowmobiles largely because of their moral commitment to environmental stewardship. Moses Lord of Fort Yukon said, "There are more dog teams around Old Crow. Now I see a lot of dog mushers. You get together and travel to communities 250 miles away. It is a lot more fun going out on a dog team. You have to spend a lot of money on gas (for snow machines). With dogs, you feed them once a day, and go 100 miles. We have up to 14 dogs in a team."

Rather than just reducing personal usage of fossil fuels, Inuit have filed suit against the biggest culprit of climate change, the United States. Citing the conclusive recent findings of U.S. government-funded scientists that climate change is having a major effect on the Arctic, the Inuit have mounted a legal challenge against the United States, which is responsible for 25 percent of global greenhouse gas emissions with only 4 percent of the world's popoulation.

The Inuit filed the challenge with the Inter-American Commission on Human Rights, part of the Organization of American States. The commission has no enforcement powers, but the *New York Times* reported that the petition has a good chance of passage, and may give a foothold for binding lawsuits to pay for climate change damage.

But Wohlforth said few he has talked to have made the moral commitment to reduce greenhouse gas emissions. "To then go the next step and say it is caused by humans is not something that everyone has been ready to do yet. And the reasons for that is simply because you have to study the science and understand it before you can be certain of that fact. Moving from that into how do we stop it, or how do we affect the change is something that I would say a small minority of people have started to do. There was a legislator who introduced a bill last year calling for Alaska to take part in mitigation efforts as far as biological mitigation. So there is a little bit."

While nuclear energy has been touted as a solution, it is not. Uranium is a non-renewable resource requiring enormous amounts of fossil fuels to mine and refine. And, nuclear waste cannot be safely contained for millions of years. Solar and wind energy are a proven solution to our energy needs.

Chris Rose of Anchorage has been working to show people that there is already proven technology today to replace fossil fuels while still meeting our energy needs. "We are going to run out of fossil fuels sooner or later," he said. "We are going to have to be planning for the next energy source anyway. So why not accelerate that planning and development so we can stop emitting carbon dioxide right now. And since we do know of technologies that are working, then why not really promote them."

The resistance from policy makers to ratifying the Kyoto Protocol has been that it could hurt the economy, Comiso said. "There could be a greater cost to the economy in getting cars to get to a certain percentage of emissions. Industrial manufacturing might feel imposed to abandon use of fossil fuels for more environmentally friendly systems.

"But it is always good to be on the safe side. We know for sure that CO_2 and other greenhouse gases emitted causes warming. We have not established one hundred percent for sure that all the change we have observed is caused by global warming. But it is always good to be on the safe side. The warming we have observed, and the regression of sea ice, and the increase of CO_2 will really make a difference on the climate. And the sooner that we can start to find an alternative, the better we will be to ensure the future of Earth's systems."

CHAPTER 27

Efficiency: Reducing Climate Change While Helping the Economy

The American economy is among the most energy-wasteful in the world. By increasing efficiency throughout our society from the personal to industrial, we can immediately help to reduce climate change emissions while also improving our economy and making us less sensitive to the costs of energy, which are expected to skyrocket as the dwindling supplies of oil and natural gas are pumped out. Efficiency will also make it far easier to transition all of our energy needs to renewable energy sources that do not cause any climate change.

Switching back to public transportation can reduce energy by 5 to 20 or more times. This has been widely known for decades. The Environmental Handbook, put out by the Friends of the Earth for the first Earth Day, April 22, 1970, reads, "If you wanted to design a transportation system to waste the earth's energy reserves and pollute the air as much as possible, you couldn't do much better than our present system dominated by the automobile.... Compared to a bus, the automobile uses from four to five times as much fuel per passenger mile. Compared to a train, it uses ten times as much. Walking and bicycling, of course, require no fuel at all. Switching from the system of auto-mobilism to a system of rapid transit, with more bicycling and walking in cities, would reduce fossil fuel consumption for transportation by a factor of almost 10."

The same is true today, and even more so with the advent of Sport Utility Vehicles (SUVs). While nearly every other country on earth is getting more efficient with its use of energy, the United States is one of the few that has gotten worse, mainly because of the popularity of gas-guzzling SUVs. Increasing public transportation opportunities and encouraging their use through advertising and subsidized fares is a very needed change.

The United States once had the greatest train system in the world. It was no accident that we changed to using automobiles to the point that now in many parts of the country one cannot travel by public transportation because it is not available. Oil and automobile companies have worked hard to dismantle public transportation, at times buying up rails lines and turning them into roads.

Gale E. Christianson writes in Greenhouse: The 200-year story of Global Warming, published in 1999 of the ruthlessness of General Motors in the 1920s to eliminate rail transportation, and eventually buses. "The lead belonged to General Motors, which was bent on exploiting its advantage by eliminating as many cheap and efficient alternatives to the automobile as possible. Starting in the 1920s, GM formed a series of holding companies that began purchasing dozens of electric surface rail transit systems throughout the country, including those in smog-free southern California, which had the largest interurban network in the land." The holding companies then scrapped the lines, forcing people to take buses or drive. Subsequently, the buses were often scrapped, so people had to drive.

"Patrons of the quiet, high-speed electrical rail service were not used to the noisy, foul-smelling buses and abandoned them by the thousands. The sales of large, fuel-hungry automobiles skyrocketed," Christianson said. And so, we are stuck in the mess of today. By switching back, to electrified rail, which is cleaner, faster and far more efficient than driving, and then electrifying the tracks with solar and wind generated electricity, we can easily move people without causing greenhouse gas emissions.

Having traveled tens of thousands of miles on the train

throughout the United States, Canada, Europe and Japan, I can attest that it is a wonderful experience, living in the lap of luxury while greatly conserving energy. One looks out a train at the landscape, without the excessive lanes of traffic, berms, guardrails and billboards of the interstate. Instead of the wasted work of driving, the stress and far greater danger, riding in a train one can work, socialize and eat a meal watching the landscape roll by. It is a quality experience instead of the chore that driving can be.

If an economist could compute the amount of wasted work time that people spend driving, that alone would be a powerful argument to switch back to public transportation. But it is our moral duty to future generations that calls upon us to make the change, and make it fast. We need politicians dedicated to investing in a massive increase in efficient public transportation and a public more eager to take the opportunities of mass transit available while demanding more from government officials.

In the meantime, raising the Corporate Average Fuel Economy (CAFE) standards is in the words of the Sierra Club, "the biggest single policy step the U.S. can take to reduce carbon dioxide emissions." We can save hundreds of times the amount of oil that could ever come from the Arctic National Wildlife Refuge by raising the CAFE standards to 39 miles per gallon, an improvement easily achievable at great benefit to the U.S. economy. Increasing fuel standards creates many times more jobs than the automated, soon to be extinct oil extraction industry. It greatly boosts all economies by increasing efficiency, while reducing our harmful impacts to the planet.

Every other sector of our energy consumption can also be greatly reduced. With electricity, switching to compact fluorescents can save 4-5 times the energy of using conventional light bulbs and they last 10 times longer, reducing the energy and resources needed to produce and replace all the incandescent light bulbs that would be saved. The same is true throughout our products, and in industrial uses as well. More insulation on homes and businesses, turning down the thermostats when no one is in a building (which can be programmed automatically) and a myriad of other, well-known methods can be used to cut our energy use enormously.

For many of us, it is a deep ethic to reduce energy consumption. When one has seen the oil field destruction of pristine wilderness, and the oily toxic mess that inevitably spills, it becomes personal. To see pristine creeks running through forest valleys turn into highwalls and strip mine destruction with acid mine drainage killing the streams and rivers brings the point home that our current energy sources are not right, and that we should avoid supporting that destruction through wasteful over-consumption. To know that we are contributing to the global catastrophe of climate change should prompt every American and world citizen to carefully consider our personal use of fossil fuels, and what we can do to reduce them.

The Environmental Handbook of 1970 states, "Many of us feel that the quality of our lives would be higher with far less use of energy in this country. We would be happy to do with fewer cars, substituting a transportation system that can make us mobile without dependence on the expensive, polluting and dangerous automobile. We would be happy to see the last of the glaring searchlights, neon signs, noisy power mowers and private airplanes, infernally noisy garbage trucks, dune buggies and motorcycles. The quality of our lives is improved by each power plant not constructed near our homes or recreation areas.... Quality of life is a positive ethic. Peace and quiet and fresh air are positive values; noisy smoking machines are negative ones."

CHAPTER 28

Winds of the Future

Just North Dakota and South Dakota alone have enough potential wind energy for the United States four times over," said Chris Rose, who works to promote renewable wind energy in Alaska. It is just a matter of distributing that energy, and developing it in places around the country. He said with the exception of the southeastern states, almost every other place in the country has viable wind resources. "We should be developing those wind resources. We can produce energy that is relatively inexpensive and emits no carbon except that which is used for the manufacture of the turbines themselves and putting them into place. Why not error on the side of caution and do something you know will decrease emissions."

"In Alaska we have a special incentive to develop renewable energy resources and that is primarily because we have 200+ remote native villages that rely on imported diesel fuel to produce their electricity. And they are paying 40-50 cents a kilowatt-hour, which is stifling their economic development and makes it real hard for them to live. So they have really been the forerunners in wind technology in this state because they have such an incentive to do it.

"There is a village of about 5,000 called Kotzebue, that is on the coast. It is in Northwest Alaska. It is the hub for all of the Northwest Arctic communities. In 1997 with the leadership of Brad Reeve, the general manager, they started to develop wind power again.

"In the early 80s, when the technology wasn't that good and the federal tax credits still existed, there was a lot of investment in wind power all over the country and especially in Alaska that failed because A) the technology was not that good and B) people were just getting the tax credits and they did not care if they operated or maintained them properly. So it left a bad taste in people's mouth about wind power.

"Back in the early 80s the cheapest you could produce wind power might have been 35 cents a kilowatt hour whereas now you can do it at three cents. So the technology has totally changed. Brad saw that in 1997 and got some money from DOE and put in a 50 kilowatt hour wind turbine that was successful and has since added them every year and now they have about 600 kilowatts of installed capacity there, and it is working great in a very harsh Arctic climate.

"It has been a stepping stone for some other villages, Wales, Gamble, Saint Paul, Port Heident, Pilot Point that already have installed wind power. And the Alaska Rural energy plan is identifying over a hundred more villages that have wind potential. So the success of the Kotzebue project has actually made people think that it is possible to do it on a larger scale here in what we call the rail belt, which is the place that we call the area between Homer and Fairbanks that is connected by electrical interties (the grid). It is essentially the same places that the Alaskan Rail line goes, but not exactly, that is why they call it the rail belt.

"That whole area is connected (by the electric grid) and Chugach Electric, which is the largest utility in the state primarily serving Anchorage, is very interested now in developing what could be a 50-100 megawatt wind farm off the coast of Anchorage on an Island called Fire Island, just a couple miles off the coast of Anchorage that could really jumpstart the harnessing of wind in Alaska.

"It would be right in the largest city in the state. If they did a hundred megawatts we would have roughly 20 percent of our load potentially served by a renewable source. That would really build enthusiasm for doing it in other places. If you look at the Department of Energy's renewable energy lab's wind atlas, they class wind in seven different classes. One is basically nonexistent; two is marginal; three is fair; four is good; five is excellent; six is outstanding; and seven is superb.

"You look at the map of the United States, there are virtually no superb wind resources anywhere in the lower 48. And if you look at a map of Alaska, the entire Alaskan Peninsula, and the Aleutian Islands and most of the coast is superb. So we've got 98-99 percent of all of the best wind resources in the whole country here.

"One of the things that we foresee happening is we are ultimately going to have to move to a hydrogen fuel cell economy at some point. It is the only energy carrier that would allow the quadrupling of energy demand on this planet that has been predicted over the next hundred years. Nothing else is going to allow us to use as much energy as we are using. Fuel cells are probably the wave of the future.

"Most of the hydrogen made in the world now is made from stripping the carbon atoms off of the hydrogen atoms from methane or natural gas. So you've got two issues with that. Number one you don't have a huge net energy gain, because you use energy to do the steam reformation process but you also have to do something with that carbon. And if you can't sequester it you have carbon emissions still.

"What we would be looking for eventually is a way to produce hydrogen in a way that does not use fossil fuels or emit any greenhouse gases. We have a way to do that if we have cheap wind power, you can use the electricity to do electrolysis. Because otherwise electrolysis doesn't have a very big net energy gain either if you use fossil fuels to run the electric current through water and make hydrogen through electrolysis, you are not gaining anything. But if you use wind energy or solar or any other renewable to make the electricity to produce the hydrogen, then you are essentially creating a full green cycle of energy because the only byproducts of a fuel cell chemical reaction is electricity, a little bit of heat and potable water. So there are no emissions from fuel cells.

"That is what we see happening in Alaska is using some of

our vast wind resources to produce hydrogen. There are already companies making fuel cell cars and fuel cell buses. In Reykjavik Iceland, the city bus drivers pull up to a Shell station that dispenses hydrogen into the fuel cell buses. And that hydrogen is being produced from electricity off Rechavick's grid that is all created by either geothermal or hydropower. They've got an electrolyzer in the Shell station, they do all of the electrolysis right there at the station. There are 80 fuel cell buses in Reykjavik now.

"Amsterdam just opened one last month. Hamburg and some other places are to open up the same thing. There are companies now that are making fuel cell cars and buses. One is New View. One of the exciting things about the Fire Island project near Anchorage is, if we could get that installed, we might be able to make some hydrogen from that wind power and have one of these same kinds of filling stations right in Anchorage. Then you could maybe convince the municipality of Anchorage to have some buses or fleet vehicles that run on hydrogen.

"Right now one of the big problems with hydrogen besides how you make it is how do you distribute it and store it. So these schemes of using the vast wind resources out on the Aleutian islands of Alaska don't make a lot of sense today because we can't economically transport that hydrogen from a place like Dutch Harbor to Tokyo. The cryogenic tankers and the things that might be used to transport liquid hydrogen or compressed hydrogen are just not economical yet. But if you can do the electrolysis right where you need it, then it makes a lot of since.

"In Reykjavik, they have that electricity right there. If we can make power in Anchorage, and make some hydrogen from it, it could work. For the next twenty years or so, you are going to have to find places close to where you have the demand to make hydrogen work.

"We as a society have not wanted to put a price on environmental degradation very often. If it costs a hundred million dollars to move the village of Shishmaref because there is less ice on the coast, because it has been melting, that is something that we might be able to attribute to this climate change.

"If it costs 35 million dollars for the state of Alaska to repair roads because the permafrost is melting, that is the kind of thing that we understand. We don't understand or put a value on species extinction. If the polar bear goes extinct in a hundred years, what will that cost. I think some economists do analyze things like existence value. That is important in the analysis in Alaska because people who might not travel to Alaska still put a value on pristine wilderness existing."

Rose said economists have put a value on ecosystem services, which are being provided by nature at 37 trillion dollars a year. "That is equal to the price of the world domestic product each year, 37 trillion dollars," he said. "Those are ways to start putting prices on things like species extinction and cultural changes."

Climate change is a major cost that is not being factored in to the price of fossil fuels, Rose said. "Since there is almost a month less river and lake ice in Alaska, that is making a difference on cultures because most people will travel more in the wintertime in rural Alaska than the summer because there is ice, and you can go places, and you can visit. A lot of places in western Alaska that have water everywhere are really hard to travel in the summer. You've got to have a boat or a plane, you can't just go by snowmobile or dogsled like you can in the winter. So if there is a month less of ice, it means there is a month less of communication between people in some instances, so that is a cultural problem.

"It is also a cultural problem if you can't eat the fish from the Yukon River or if you can't find the other foods that you would normally find because of ecosystem changes. So the externalities are not counted at all.

"These are externalities that are finally being measured, but the connection is not being made by most average folks. That is an important thing to consider. What happens if we can't live the way we used to live. That is not a question that most people are considering. But it is a huge externality.

"The other thing about the prices, one of the things that is really important for wind energy development still is the 1.7 cents per kilowatt-hour production tax credit, the PTC the federal government gives to for-profit utility companies for producing wind. Even without the 1.7 cents per kilowatt-hour subsidy, we are still looking at very competitive wind projects in the lower 48. The PTC is essentially there because Congress feels that wind has to be given some equal footing because the other energy sectors get subsidies."

Concern that the PTC would not be renewed was in part responsible for the slowdown of new wind energy production in the United States from 1635 megawatts in 2001 to 429 megawatts in 2002. Rose said Bush's energy policy has been to further subsidize polluting fossil fuel industries instead of investing in solar or wind.

"The energy bill that failed (in 2003) had billions of dollars in subsidies for the oil and gas industries. When we are looking at policy it is important to consider who is getting what. It is amazing to me that the tax deduction that an average person gets if they get a Prius went down last year from $2,000 to $1,500 but if I want to go out an buy a 6,000 pound Hummer that gets 8 miles per gallon, I would be able to write the entire $60,000 off. It is crazy."

Taxpayers for Common Sense agreed, noting that purchasers can take $106,000 off their taxes of the $110,000 purchase price of the most expensive Hummer, and that businesses can also write off the purchase of SUVs from their taxes. The group issued a statement December 12 2003 stating, "The tax exemption has become a misguided incentive for people to buy much larger vehicles than they need."

Rose continued, "Policies are really important. I am looking at what we can do in Alaska to provide some more policy incentives for renewables. One of the interesting things that we might be able to do up here is to get interested companies involved in what is going on in the bush because those little villages need much different kinds of wind turbines than the big utility sized ones that are being proposed for Fire Island or that are being used in the lower 48 in wind farms because these villages might only have a hundred people, they don't need a huge turbine.

"Some of the big turbines are large enough now that they can electrify three thousand homes with one turbine. Obviously you don't need that kind of thing in a small village. But the companies that might want to get involved and continue to make the smaller turbines might be able to market those same kinds of systems to the developing world where there are a lot of places that still don't have electricity. The whole idea of leapfrogging technology comes into play. There are lots of places in Africa that are never going to have phone lines, because they didn't have phones, and cell phones got invented, and now people are getting cell phones. They will never have telephone lines there.

"The same thing could happen with electricity if they could find a way to create electricity in their area with renewables. They would not necessarily have to be connected to the grid. Which has all of its own downfalls as we saw last October (2003) with the power outages. The more you are connected, the more vulnerable you are in many ways. If you have what's called distributed generation where you can produce power more locally, you have a little more control over what is going on."

Eventually wind and solar on the grid would help to reduce blackouts, Rose said, but only after a massive increase in their usage. "We are so reliant on centrally generated electricity. The answer is yes (it would make us less vulnerable to blackouts) but it would take a long time.

"If we had a hundred percent wind in this country, we would still have to have some transmission lines, because the wind does not always blow all the time. So we still have to have some transmission lines, because if the wind wasn't blowing in Avaline, Texas one day, they would have to get their wind power from somewhere in Oklahoma maybe, because the wind does not always blow one hundred percent of the time.

"For instance in Denmark, they are up to where twenty percent of their electricity is being generated by wind right now. And what they are finding is the more places that they put the wind generators, the more stable their wind grid is becoming, because the wind might be blowing in place A but not place B.

With a more serious investment in wind energy, Rose said "it wouldn't take long for these industries to develop. There is all kind of information out there, and analysis and predictions of how much spending would do what. Even a relatively modest in the greater scheme of things investment of a hundred billion dollars over a period of years would be a huge boost to the renewable energy economy. A hundred billion dollars is not that much when you consider that we are spending four hundred billion dollars a year on our military right now.

"People have to accept the argument that a big portion of that is to protect Persian Gulf oil access. So why don't we take some of the money from our military budget and from oil and gas and put it toward subsidies and incentives for renewables, or hydrogen fuel cell research and we wouldn't have to protect our Persian Gulf oil. It really is not that much money in the greater scheme of things.

"If you ask me whether I like paying a dollar eighty a gallon for gas I would say I think we should pay at the pump what it really is costing our country because in Europe they are paying five dollars a gallon, and I would argue that here we are paying much closer to five dollars a gallon than we think because much of those costs are downstream in higher taxes to support things like the military that protects our oil. Even though we are not paying five dollars at the pump, there's other hidden costs in our economy like the military budget that are attributable to our dependence on fossil fuels. It wouldn't take a lot.

"There are a lot more jobs in the renewable and the efficiencies areas than there are in oil and gas. A lot of oil and gas are automated technologies and there aren't a lot of people involved. But if you just look at efficiency, economists and folks who look at the stuff believe that by the year 2010, we could reduce our energy by 10 percent if we just introduce some efficiency measures, and twenty percent by 2020 if we did the same thing. You can create a lot more jobs as well if you hire a bunch of people to retrofit lighting and tune up air conditioners and things like that than you do in just producing more oil.

"I know there is a lot of job potential (in solar and wind). And they're sustainable jobs. That's the thing about a lot of these jobs is they will last forever, because the wind is going to keep blowing. You are going to have to keep putting new turbines up and maintain them. But the oil jobs and the gas jobs whether it is in 20 years or 100 years, they will go away. One of the big topic of discussion up here is what are we going to do with our fiscal gap.

"I just got back from a two-day conference in Anchorage called Alaska 2020 which is a visionary kind of process of where are we going to be in 2020. One of the big issues that came up at this conference is we don't have a very diversified economy. Two-thirds of our economy up here is either Ted Stevens giving us money because he is the chair of appropriations, or oil revenue. Both of those things are going to end.

"We really need to look at diversification. And we have the ability to continue to be an energy state; we just have to use our brains around the idea of being a different kind of energy state."

While some have complained about altering natural viewsheds with wind generators, Rose said, "To me, it is a visible sign of progress that we would have our energy generated by renewable energy sources. And the fact is we don't see the emissions that are being created by the burning of fossil fuels for electricity so it is out of sight and out of mind. I think it is nice to see where your electricity comes from.

"I do think that there are places that are very special that we should consider the viewshed of. But for the most part, I don't have a problem with the viewshed issue. We have worked with the conservation community in Anchorage to develop support for the Fire Island project. In fact we even developed support for a smaller pilot project with wind energy that Chugach electric was considering in Chugach State Park, right in one of the most beautiful viewshed in the state in a fjord right south of Anchorage.

"We even got support from the conservation community to do that because we realized that the tradeoffs are so important. On Fire Island, it s not going to be a big issue because it is far enough off shore, nobody lives on it, and it is not going to be a viewshed issue. Even if it was a viewshed issue, I think people would be Ok with it because the conservation community here in Anchorage realizes how important it is to begin to wean ourselves of fossil fuels.

"You can see it and say 'Wow, look at that.' We were even considering having a Kiosk right there explaining what it is all about and get people excited instead of just assuming people are going to just like it. A lot of people have seen Altamont Pass in California which was one of the first big wind developments in our country. Those places were both sited poorly. First of all, they killed a lot of raptors, because they sited them on ridgelines where the raptors fly and they killed a lot of birds. Secondly, they have continued to kind of add haphazardly to what they started with.

"Even though they started with what would be considered today tiny little turbines, they've begun to add the really big ones and it is a very hodgepodge look. With the new wind farms that are being created today in Iowa and Minnesota and Oregon, they're just putting up these huge, sleek turbines. They all look the same. The blades are so big that they actually turn slower, and they make less noise.

"It is not the hodge-podge look that you get in Altamont Pass in California. They are all big, and there are fewer of them because they are much, much bigger. They will still kill birds. What is happening though is people are getting smarter about where to site them. If you put a new wind turbine in a bad place, it is still going to kill a lot of birds.

"What they are doing is doing more pre-construction studies to see where the birds are, and then doing more monitoring afterwards. They are doing a lot less damage to the avian population just because of better planning. And you also have to put that into perspective. There are an estimated one billion birds killed each year from manmade structures. One billion, and 80 million by house cats. And about 40-60,000 birds are killed a year by wind turbines. So it is a really tiny amount of birds.

"What people are still concerned about, and rightly so are raptors, and endangered species. So when Fish and Wildlife Service are helping people to site a wind farm, those are the things that they are looking for: raptors and endangered species.

"The other thing that has changed to make fewer bird kills, is now we have these tubular towers, instead of the lattice type towers. The lattice type tower attracted birds for nesting because they had a place to sit. So it is better to have the tubular towers where there is no place to nest or roost and hang out. That is another difference.

"The tip speed is still pretty fast. The rotor speed is slower. But way out there on the tip it is moving fast. It is still moving pretty fast but it is not moving as fast as the smaller blades. They are also experimenting with different things like lights and colors and things like that. Lights are found to attract birds, at least certain color lights, so it appears that lights are not good. I think that most of the decrease in kills is figuring out what birds you've got before you build it so then you can design and locate it in areas where it doesn't affect them as much.

"Viewsheds and birds, those are the big issues with wind power I think. And I don't think they are that big, but they are issues. I think energy is the most important issue. It affects everything. It affects our environment, it affects our economy, it affects our geopolitical policy. So it is the most important issue in my mind for any politician at the national level to be focusing on."

CHAPTER 29

Solar Powering the World

Having helped to build a home that ran entirely off solar and wind energy near Athens, Ohio, where we were told it was too cloudy and not windy enough, and seeing it easily power the living of 11 people who lived in the home, I am convinced that both offer the solution to our energy needs. It was actually cheaper to build a solar and wind home than to pay the cost of extending the power lines to the house. And that was in 1994.

Like computers and VCRs, the costs are plummeting for solar and wind energy, making them cost-competitive with fossil fuel energy production, and not even taking into account the externality pollution costs that make renewable energy vastly cheaper than their fossil competitors in the long run.

With a battery bank and the constancy of solar and wind energy, our lights never went out. Meanwhile, our neighbors, who ran on coal-generated electricity that fed into the grid they were on, had regular power outages. The coal industry lied with their propaganda that "coal keeps the lights on," plastered on billboards and media advertisements.

But the truth was that our lights were powered cheaper with solar and wind even in the skewed economics of our day that falsely favors fossil fuels (Ohio gives $3 to coal companies for every ton of coal mined in the state). It was our solar and wind power system that kept the lights on. Meanwhile, the coal industry lights regularly failed, while contributing to the death of the planet through climate change, acid rain, mercury pollution, particulate pollution, acid mine drainage, strip mining and mountaintop removal devastation and more.

The amount of solar energy available on earth is so much that in one minute, the equivalent energy is received by Earth as the world uses in an entire year. But different parts of the world have different amounts of solar energy based on the season, elevation and cloud cover. The solar energy industry touts solar energy as being:

- Proven commercial technology
- Highly reliable
- Low in operating costs
- Minimal in servicing and requiring no refueling
- Of modular design and mobile
- Globally applicability from the Tropics to the Arctic
- Easily mass produced and installed
- Creates clean, sustainable jobs.

Just a small fraction of our south facing rooftops is all of the energy that we need. A new study revealed by Princeton University in September, 2003 found that they could produce organic solar energy cells, as opposed to the inorganic silicon cells now widely used. While the efficiency would not be as great for these cells, the costs would be so vastly cheaper as to make the overall wattage far cheaper. They could be made in many colors, even transparent sheets that could be used as tinting for windows while producing energy. This multi-coloring and ultra-thin design means it could easily be incorporated into highly aesthetic and diverse architectural buildings.

A British Petroleum study in 1997 found that an investment of $550 million into a 500-megawatt solar photovoltaic factory would lower the production cost of solar panels by 80 percent. BP found that using existing technology in 1997, a large-scale factory can be built with no barriers to reach 500 megawatt per year production of photovoltaic modules using crystalline silicon. That is less than 700 times smaller than the annual U.S. military budget. And, improved technology since 1997 has made the cost even lower.

The *San Francisco Chronicle* reported that solar energy power production is growing 30 percent a year. The fastest growing sector in the industry is installing solar photovoltaic rooftop arrays on businesses, which recoup the costs in four to eight years. Systems today are half the cost of systems seven years ago, reported Daniel Shugar, president of PowerLight, a Berkeley, California firm that installs solar systems. Every three years the solar energy industry doubles, and with that doubling of volume, prices are reduced 18 percent. Just a thousandth of the U.S. Defense budget put into producing solar power would double the growth of the industry.

Today, Japan, Germany and California lead in the global solar market, with 40 percent of solar production now in Japan, 20 percent in Germany and 12 percent in the United States. The industry is waiting for a Henry Ford of the solar energy business to streamline and reduce the costs even further. U.S. Department of Energy spokesperson David Garman said that the DOE is committed to reducing the manufacturing costs of solar photovoltaic cell modules to $3 per watt by 2010, and $1.50 per watt by 2020.

While President Jimmy Carter put solar panels on the White House, President Ronald Reagan took them off. "President" George Bush put solar panels on a shed in 2003 in a token gesture of eco-consciousness that was only window dressing for an administration with the most anti-environmental record ever. In policy, Bush has worked to remove subsidies from solar and wind energy, and put subsidies on the fossil fuel industry, which funded his "election" campaign.

"If you have more renewables, you will create more jobs, you will decrease our dependence on foreign oil which in turn will perhaps make our relations with other countries better,"

Rose said. "And we know that we are going to be reducing our output of greenhouse gases which would have a huge effect on our civilization ultimately."

Individuals can take actions in their own lives to reduce greenhouse gas emissions, particularly in the United States where we use so much fossil-fuel energy, Rose said. "Buy a hybrid car. Do more carpooling, do more walking. Replace lights with energy efficient lighting. Replace appliances like air conditioners and refrigerators and clothes driers with more efficient models. Educate themselves about what is going on around the world both as a result of emissions of greenhouse gases but also about the solutions. They should urge their utility companies to use renewable energy sources to generate electricity.

"People can demand from their local utility that they have the opportunity to buy some portion of green power. So there are a lot of things that individuals can do. We in the United States especially need to consider how much energy we are using. We take it for granted when we get on a plane or drive a car. But we are not really connecting that use of fossil fuel to what is going on with climate change. I think if we all educate ourselves a little more, we wouldn't want to do some of the things that we're doing and we'd all want to do the right thing.

"We all have an inner instinct to conserve and to do the right thing, but we aren't making the connection. We aren't using fossil fuels an armload at a time like when we are filling our wood stove with the trees that we cut up and sawed up. So we don't have that connection to the fuel that we're using. We don't see the tankers that supply our gas. We don't see the gas line going into our house. So it is out of sight, out of mind. I think we need to find more ways to develop the measuring eye that we have with simple fuels like wood.

"There is a sign in Manhattan that displays our national debt continuously. Why can't we have a sign that displays how much fossil fuel we are using? Why can't the little monitors in the hybrid car that tells you your real-time mileage (the miles per gallon as it varies during your driving), why can't those be standard equipment in all cars, so if you are only getting eight miles per gallon it is right in your face? Those are the kinds of things I think we need to put two and two together."

We know the solutions. We have the technology to do it. It is imperative that we realize our power as citizens to make a difference and change our government and industries to reduce greenhouse gas emissions. The fossil fuel industry, with its billions of dollars and entrenched desire to keep the status quo of destruction, has a clear advantage. But we cannot let the difficulty of our task get in the way of our action. There are millions of people around the world deeply concerned about climate change, and dedicated to making a difference.

The seriousness of this issue begs every citizen today to get active politically to institute the needed changes in government policy that would reduce our emissions of greenhouse gases instead of increasing them. We must demand that our policymakers invest in fuel-efficient trains, mass transit and bicycle lanes instead of polluting airplanes and highways, and mandate efficiency in cars, trucks and appliances. We must demand that subsidies for fossil fuels be replaced by subsidies for solar and wind energy.

The fate of the world is in our hands: the people in this pivotal time. It is up to us to make the future a living one. That means changing our present course, dramatically. It means changing our priorities. We need an army of activists dedicated to nonviolent social change through political involvement on a daily basis. It us up to us to be the difference, if the diversity of life as we know it is to survive.

This is the ultimate issue of our time. Future generations will be very critical of those who argue for the continued use of coal and oil. The pioneers of the solar and wind energy generation will be seen as the heroes of our day. We must make the change and invest in our future, before it is too late.

Part Three

THE ARCTIC REFUGE

The Back Side of the Moon or the Last Great Refuge?
What the Oil Company Victory Means for the Arctic

Sitting atop the northern face of the Brooks Mountain Range at Sunset Pass in August, 2004, I overlooked the coastal plain of the Arctic National Wildlife Refuge which stretched far to the east and west, and north to the blue waters of the Arctic Ocean and far out to the pack ice scores of miles from shore. To have an all-natural landscape with pure untouched and undamaged rivers and streams from the headwaters high in the mountains where I now sit, all the way to the ocean is one of the most important of treasures left.

Caribou were migrating from the plain back toward their wintering grounds over the mountains. One ran right up to us, a husky male with a giant rack. Seeing us, he snorted and bolted back, then ran far around. I had just stayed with the Gwich'in people who have lived off the caribou for tens of thousands of years, interviewing them for an upcoming book, and boated 300 miles down the Porcupine River with two Gwich'in guides. The importance of this place cannot fully be told in words. There is just a deep, unquestionable perfection in the complete, working ecosystem, and the words and charisma of the Gwich'in peoples living as part of it.

The Arctic National Wildlife Refuge contains the last five percent of protected North Slope of Alaska: the coastal plain. From a range the size of California, caribou migrate across the Brooks Mountain Range to mass together on the coastal plain and give birth to the next generation of caribou.

But these are the most dire of days for those of us who know and understand the importance of the great Arctic National Wildlife Refuge to be left as wilderness. The March 16, 2005 51-49 vote in the U.S. Senate to keep drilling in the Arctic Refuge in the budget bill was done against the will of the vast majority of the American people, and with lies and backdoor political maneuvers that subvert the democratic process of our great nation.

Scientists Speak for Refuge Protection

More than a thousand U.S. and Canadian scientists called on President Bush to protect the Arctic National Wildlife Refuge from oil drilling on February 14, 2005. In a letter to the President, the scientists questioned assertions that oil could be safely extracted from the Refuge, and urged President Bush to "support permanent protection of the coastal plain's significant wildlife and wilderness values."

The scientists found that oil development could seriously harm caribou, polar bears, muskoxen and snow geese—among other wildlife. They warned it could disrupt the fragile ecosystem of the coastal plain, which could lead to more widespread injury to wildlife and its habitat. The signers categorically rejected the notion that the impacts of drilling could be confined to a limited footprint, as pro-drilling forces claim, noting that the effects of oil wells, pipelines, roads, airports, housing facilities, processing plants, gravel mines, air pollution, industrial noise, seismic exploration and exploratory drilling would radiate across the entire coastal plain of the Arctic Refuge.

Defenders of Wildlife President Rodger Schlickeisen said, "hundreds of scientists are telling President Bush that throwing the Arctic National Wildlife Refuge open to oil companies will harm wildlife and permanently disrupt the wild nature of this unique place. It simply does not make sense to destroy the Arctic Refuge for oil that won't lower prices and won't make a noticeable dent in our dependency on foreign energy, when it's so much easier to get the same amount of energy through common-sense conservation steps."

The "2,000" Acre Lie

President George Bush says drilling would take only a

2,000-acre footprint. That's a postage stamp in one of the world's largest wilderness areas. Unfortunately, his statement is a lie. The legislation to open the refuge in the budget bill would lease all million and a half acres of the coastal plain, unleashing sprawling industrial development throughout the area. The plain is the biological heart of the Arctic Refuge, an intact ecosystem that remains entirely natural, comprising one hundred million acres. By destroying the heart, the whole will die.

The so-called directional drilling improvements that theoretically will constrain the sprawl are far more propaganda than fact: they have only decreased the size of drill pads by 10 percent in 30 years, and oil spills are increasing. More than 500 oil spills occur every year: more than one a day. The consequences are now becoming clear: the National Academy of Sciences found that drilling around Prudhoe Bay had a negative impact on the caribou, bowhead whale and almost every other wildlife species.

As I described in my earlier book, Arctic Quest, I've seen this devastation first hand. I backpacked hundreds of miles through the oil fields of Prudhoe Bay, and into the Arctic National Wildlife Refuge in 1991. Prudhoe Bay is an industrial nightmare with massive development and toxic waste spread over more than a thousand square miles and for scores of miles in all directions. They have dredged enough gravel to fill 90,000 football fields to a height of 3 feet for all of this development. There are gravel roads all over, gigantic pumping stations and a massive network of roads. Dredging for gravel is done in rivers and streams and devastates their ecology.

The Alaskan North slope existing oil development has more than 4,800 exploratory and production wells, 223 production and exploratory drill pads, more than 500 miles of roads, 1,800 miles of pipes over 600 miles of pipeline corridors, two refineries, 20 airports, 107 gravel pads for living quarters and other support facilities, five docks and gravel causeways, 36 gravel mines, 28 production plants, gas processing facilities, seawater treatment plants and power plants.

Oil companies caused more than 4,532 spills between 1996 and 2004 totaling more than 1.9 million gallons of toxic substances. The most commonly spilled pollutants are diesel, crude and hydraulic oil. More than forty different toxic wastes have been spilled across a thousand square miles in all directions from Prudhoe Bay. The number of spills has been dramatically increasing, from an average of 400 spills per year in 2000 to an average of more than 550 spills per year in 2004.

Air pollution around Prudhoe Bay exceeds that of Washington, DC, and nitrogen dioxide levels are twice that of DC. The oil industry emits 70,000 tons of nitrogen oxides, which cause acid rain and smog, 6,199 tons of particulate matter, 1,470 tons of sulfur dioxide, 11,560 tons of carbon monoxide, 2,647 tons of volatile organic compounds, 24,000 metric tons of methane and up to 40 million metric tons of carbon dioxide annually.

The oil companies already have 95 percent of the North Slope, and now they are trying to destroy the last bit of remaining wilderness.

Proponents argue the costs are worth it: we can cut our dependence on foreign oil. But it would take at least ten years to see oil from the Arctic Refuge to market according to the General Accounting Office (GAO). The agency also found the refuge would provide such an insignificant amount that it would have virtually no impact on the price of oil and would only increase U.S. production by 2-3 percent at its peak, up to 20 years after development would start.

Increasing the Corporate Average Fuel Economy (CAFE) standards to 39 miles per gallon, however, would save more than 100 times the oil than would ever come from the Arctic National Wildlife Refuge. In fact, more oil would be saved in increasing the CAFE standards than is in the Arctic National Wildlife Refuge before even a drop of oil from the refuge would get to market.

Such a change in standards would have a big impact on the Refuge and create far more jobs in retooling the auto industry compared to the few automated oil industry jobs if the refuge were to be opened. But it would have zero impact on people's lifestyles, except to save them money on gas. With Ford having come out with an SUV hybrid-electric vehicle getting 39 miles per gallon, this could easily be done without impacting peoples choice of vehicle. Mid-sized cars can easily get 50-70 mpg.

Meanwhile, the impact of drilling on the lifestyles of those living in the Arctic National Refuge will be huge. These caribou feed 17 Gwich'in villages. The Gwich'in are caribou people, who have lived for 30,000 years off the Porcupine Caribou Herd that calves on the coastal plain, right where they want to drill for oil. These are among the last native peoples on Earth whose culture we have not yet destroyed.

This is the densest area for polar bear dens in the world, home to one of the last refuges of muskox, grizzly bear, Arctic wolves, Arctic fox, and much more. This is not just some place way up North, it affects everyone in every state of the U.S. and 6 continents around the world. More than 160 species of birds from 6 continents and all 50 states breed on the coastal plain of the Arctic National Wildlife Refuge.

But the refuge has never been more threatened than now. All could be lost if drilling is passed in the budget bill now before Congress. If drilling is approved, and we lose in the court battles that would ensue, this last refuge will be gone forever. To compare the Arctic National Wildlife Refuge to the backside of the moon, as pro-drilling Senator Larry Craig, a Republican from Idaho did in March, 2005, is like comparing life and death. The Arctic Refuge is among the last places on Earth with all of its original inhabitants still intact. All of the plants and animals that were there are still there, making it among the most important areas in the world to protect.

Fuzzy Math

Because drilling proponents cannot open the Arctic Refuge through the proper process, they snuck it in the budget bill where it does not belong. This issue has nothing to do with the budget: this is just a backdoor way to get drilling approved, because the budget bill cannot be filibustered.

The budget bill included $4,000-$6,000 in revenues per acre for what they expect to receive by leasing land in the Arctic National Wildlife Refuge to oil companies. In fact drilling leases have on average gone for $50 an acre in the North Slope of Alaska. And leases to drill in the Arctic National Wildlife Refuge promise to be much different than leases throughout the rest of the coastal plain. A senior Bush Administration official told the New York Times that they probably could not give away leases to drill in the Arctic National Wildlife Refuge. Environmental groups promise an immediate boycott and campaign against any company that would bid on such leases.

On February 24, 2005, Representatives Tom Allen, a Democrat from Maine, Massachusetts Democrat Edward Markey and California Democrat Lois Capps demanded to know the economic basis for the extremely high figures for the price of leasing land in the Arctic National Wildlife Refuge to oil companies. The assumptions were 80-120 times the average lease fees paid by oil companies, and is an example of fuzzy math from an administration that distorts the facts to pass unpopular legislation to benefit the oil companies that it represents.

Senator Olympia Snowe, a Republican from Maine said "we believe the projected revenues appear to fall far short of realistic leasing figures. Accordingly, we strongly believe that the nation's budget should not be founded, even in part, on such speculative and unrealistic revenue projections."

Groups Promise Court Battle and Corporate Campaign if Congress Approves Drilling

But all of this presumes passage of drilling in the budget, which is now pending as this goes to press. If it does pass Congress, an unprecedented coalition of environmental groups promises an unprecedented volley of lawsuits to protect the refuge from the many violations of laws that drilling in the refuge would create. International treaties to protect the Porcupine Caribou Herd, the Endangered Species Act, the National Environmental Protection Act and many more laws would be violated with Congressional approval to drill in the Arctic National Wildlife Refuge.

If drilling is passed by Congress, Alaska Wilderness League National Field Director Erik Dumont emphasized that activists will not give up the struggle. "There's two options, obviously one is through the courts, using the legal system to challenge the validity of the sale on a number of grounds. There are several treaties that we have that would protect the caribou herd: the treaty with Canada and others. We also have a treaty to protect the polar bears. Either one of which could be used as grounds for lawsuits.

"Also there would be a corporate campaign aimed at any companies that would bid on any lease sales. Some people are already doing it—they are not waiting to do corporate campaigns—to push them back from the support they have shown already for drilling in the Arctic."

If drilling is passed, Dumont said that activists would "definitely not" give up the struggle, but instead would escalate the campaign. "It seems that with every setback we've had, some of our more fervent activists, even more than before have dug in their heals. This really sucks what they just did and it makes us that much more committed to make sure we don't lose down the road. I don't think that losing here or any other particular place would make anybody give up. Certainly not us anyway."

Opening the Floodgates: The Arctic is Just The Beginning

In 2005, Conoco-Phillips joined BP in pulling out of Arctic Power, the lead lobbying group to open the Arctic Refuge. With Alaska's two largest oil companies no longer interested in drilling in the Arctic Refuge, many question the Bush Administration's zeal to open the refuge. But the benefits to oil companies for passage of drilling in the refuge extend well beyond any windfall in the Arctic. As one proponent of drilling said, opening the refuge would "break the back of the environmental movement," and open up the coasts of Florida and California to drilling, where there is a significant amount of oil.

On March 17, 2005, Senator Ken Salazar, a Democrat from Colorado, said, "last night on the Senate floor, I continued my determined fight to say to our children and grandchildren that we will protect certain pristine areas of this great country. The Arctic National Wildlife Refuge is one of those places." He said that the Arctic National Wildlife Refuge is "a refuge from encroachment and a symbol of restraint and our optimism for the future. Today I voted for an amendment to protect the refuge, and yet it is with a heavy heart that I write this statement with one of our last remaining wilderness areas under siege, threatened to be opened up for exploration and drilling for a six-month supply of oil. This move would set an ominous precedent."

Senator Salazar continued, "The Coloradans and Americans alike should know that once this door is unlocked it will be that much easier to unhinge the protections of every refuge from the Alamosa National Wildlife Refuge in my home San Luis Valley to the Florida Everglades Wildlife Refuge. From the purple mountains majesty to the coasts of our shining seas. It is my hope that we can demonstrate to the American public our commitment to future generations through protecting pristine lands. We owe it to our children as a compact to the generations beyond."

Polls Show Overwhelming Public Opposition to Oil Development

There is a pervasive picture of Americans as gas guzzlers who just don't care about the environment, and that it is the general public that is pressuring politicians to get oil cheaply, regardless of environmental costs. It's a convenient scapegoat:

blame the general public. But on this issue, most Americans see the facts clearly—and they don't like what they see.

A bipartisan national survey found that by a margin of 58 to 33 percent, Americans oppose proposals to drill for oil in the Arctic National Wildlife Refuge, according to U.S. Newswire, February 9, 2005. The bipartisan telephone poll of 1,003 registered voters was conducted January 13-17, 2005. Almost twice as many people opposed drilling than favored it.

A Democratic and a Republican polling firm teamed up to do the national poll. Democratic polling firm Lake, Snell, Perry and Associates Spokesperson Celinda Lake said, "Voters believe there are some places that should simply be off limits to oil drilling and the Arctic Refuge is one of them. They believe we have a moral responsibility to protect this unique area, and the abundant birds and wildlife that live there for future generations."

The spokesperson for the Republican polling firm, Bellwether Research and Consulting, Christine Matthews said "one of the most striking findings from this poll is the degree to which voter opinion on this issue of drilling in the Arctic Refuge has solidified, moving from the realm of public policy issue to value. Only about ten percent of Americans are undecided on this issue—most people know where they stand when it comes to drilling in the Arctic National Wildlife Refuge.

Far more than the number who opposed drilling, A resounding 73 percent of Americans said that the issue of drilling in the Arctic Refuge is too important to the American public and future generations to be snuck through in the budget process, and disagree with drilling proponents' arguments in favor of allowing drilling to be determined in the budget. Even among Republicans and those who voted for George Bush in 2004, a majority oppose using the budget process to open the Arctic Refuge to oil drilling. The opposition is consistent across age, gender, party and other demographic groups. Dozens of other national polls over the last two decades have found a vast majority support refuge protection.

This photo is of the upper watershed of the Canning River in the Arctic Refuge from the bush plane the author flew in over the Brooks Mountain Range in 1994. Photo by Myra Keeter.

All That Destruction for a Drop in the Bucket?

A statement released November 11, 2004 by the Alaska Coalition, Alaska Wilderness League, Appalachian Voices, Defenders of Wildlife, Earthjustice, Gwich'in Steering Committee, National Audubon Society, National Wildlife Federation, Northern Alaska Environmental Center, Sierra Club, Trustees for Alaska, U.S. Public Interest Research Group, the Wilderness Society and World Wildlife Fund stated:

"The Arctic National Wildlife Refuge is under threat again. Nevertheless, as they have before, Americans will once again rise up and speak out for thoughtful conservation of the Arctic Refuge.

"The Bush Administration and its allies in Congress have made it clear that their shortsighted energy policy will continue to give inflated prominence to drilling in the Arctic National Wildlife Refuge. Despite the fact that drilling in the Arctic has twice been rejected by bipartisan majorities in the

Senate, and that a majority of the American public does not support it, the Bush administration continues to push this unpopular initiative.

"No matter how many times the administration tried to advance this plan, the facts haven't changed: drilling in the Arctic National Wildlife Refuge would ruin one of America's last unspoiled wild places for what the U.S. Geological Survey and oil company executives admit is only a few months' worth of oil that would not be available for a decade. The American people don't want that, and they've made that clear.

"Proponents of drilling in the Arctic Refuge have a much broader agenda—just last year, Representative Tom DeLay told a group of high-ranking Republicans that the controversy over drilling in the Arctic National Wildlife Refuge is a "symbolic" debate about whether or not oil and gas drilling should be allowed in pristine wild areas across the country.

"Ultimately, the battle over the Arctic Refuge says a lot about what sort of nation we are going to be. Are we a country that squanders its natural resources for short-term profit? Or are we a nation that stewards those resources, carefully conserving the most valuable natural and economic assets to ensure we will have them in the future?

"For some five decades, thousands of citizens from all walks of life and all areas of the nation have worked to protect the Arctic Refuge. Leaders of both political parties have recognized the importance of protecting the area. President Dwight Eisenhower established the Arctic National Wildlife Range in 1960. It was enlarged by President Jimmy Carter in 1980. Backed by the majority of American people, bipartisan majorities in the US Senate have voted time and again to keep the oil drills out of the Refuge's Coastal Plain.

"Protecting the Arctic Refuge is important ecologically and culturally. The narrow Coastal Plain is the foundation of a delicate ecosystem that features a spectacular diversity of wildlife, including hundreds of bird species, polar bears, musk

East fork of the Chandaler River in the southern portion of the Arctic National Wildlife Refuge.

oxen and wolves. The area also supports the Porcupine Caribou Herd, which calves on the Coastal Plain. The caribou are the basis of the subsistence culture of the Gwich'in people, whose communities lie along the migration route of the herd."

"The facts demonstrate that the existing reserve within the refuge has a total potential of providing only the amount of oil consumed by the United States in six months" said Senator Ken Salazar, a Democrat from Colorado. "By the year 2015, developing the refuge and extracting the oil will reduce U.S. reliance on foreign oil sources by 1 percent from 63 percent to 62 percent... That is why opening the Arctic National Wildlife Refuge is only a one percent solution to the energy challenge that is strangling America today. Indeed, the energy challenge requires our attention to embrace a new covenant of conservation including fuel efficiency and development of alternative fuels like wind, ethanol and solar power."

"The fact is the price of oil will not drop, the price of energy will not drop, the price of gasoline will not drop, because with three percent of the oil reserves of the world in our hands including Alaska, you can't drill your way out of America's predicament," said Senator John Kerry in March, 2005.

"Sacred places need to be protected" began a column in The North Wind, Northern Michigan University's college paper, February 28, 2005 by David Moss. "A refuge's main mission is 'preserving unique wildlife, wilderness and recreational values,' according to the Arctic National Wildlife Refuge web site.

"Establishment of oil wells certainly won't help preserve wildlife, and the last thing I want to encounter on a recreational trip into the wilderness is an oil rig. How then can Bush justify his continued zeal to rob this area of its innocence? To save a few pennies at the pump?

"I can assure you opening the wildlife refuge to drilling won't make a noticeable difference at the gas pumps. Oil wells are a simple fix to a greater problem. Cheaper energy can only come from conservation and alternative sources that don't rely on dwindling supplies of fossil fuels.

The key is in conservation and investing in renewable energy sources like solar and wind. With just a fraction of our military budget invested over a few decades, we could be entirely powered by clean solar and wind energy. As we invest more and more in solar and wind, we can replace the inevitably declining supplies of fossil fuels, that we really should not be burning anyway. Exponentially more people than died in the terrorist attacks of September 11, 2001 would be saved every year in the United States from the pollution that would be eliminated if we were to do that. Tens of thousands more lives would be saved by switching from gas guzzling and dangerous automobile transport to super-energy efficient and safe public transportation.

Creating a Wasteland to Cure a Senator's Clinical Depression?: The Forces Behind the Drilling

Alaskan Republican Senator Ted Stevens said that he was clinically depressed over his efforts to drill in the refuge. With his decades-long effort to destroy this last intact caribou herd left in the United States and this last native culture living off an undisturbed ecosystem, one wonders if this was a Freudian slip for this lead proponent of drilling in this area that must be protected as wilderness. With 95 percent of the North Slope already open to oil development, Senator Stevens must have it all, and will be shunned by future generations as among the last dinosaur of anti-environmental imperialists. We must make such politicians extinct now by getting more political, and collectively voting them out of office.

"The easiest thing the average person can do is use less fuel," Moss wrote. "This might mean retiring the unnecessary sports utility vehicle and other gas guzzlers in exchange for smaller, more practical and efficient vehicles."

"If only the billions of dollars spent thus far by companies on getting ANWR oil could be reinvested in alternative energies, maybe some real progress could be made."

While demented politicians have claimed drilling in the Arctic Refuge could somehow make us safer from terrorism, by providing more domestic oil, it in fact would increase the risk of terrorism, as it would put more of our energy supply through 700 miles of extreme vulnerability: The Trans Alaskan Pipeline. A drunk hunter shot a hole through the pipeline in October, 2001, spilling 285,000 gallons of oil. Crude oil gushed out of the pipe at a hundred gallons a minute, spraying for hundreds of feet. The one bullet shut down the pipeline for a week. That is not a secure way to get our energy. Solar and wind, however, are decentralized and an energy source that is very secure from terrorism.

A Time for Action Over Despair

I have been traveling all around the country, from Texas to New York and Washington State to Florida doing slide presentations about my journey through the Arctic National Wildlife Refuge with the Alaska Wilderness League and the Alaska Coalition. I have been educating people about the habitat, the people who live there, and what is at stake.

As could be expected, I listened to every news cast I could

Oil gushes from the Trans Alaskan Pipeline after a drunk hunter shot it in October 2001—not a safe way to get our energy. Photo courtesy of the Alaska Wilderness League.

(made far greater with high speed internet), watched every broadcast and read every article that I could about the threat to the beloved wilderness that I feel deeply attached to. Reliving my journey through the refuge night after night, with my Arctic photos projected in front of me day after day, and meeting people around the country working on this issue constantly reminds me of the urgent need for citizen action to save the great refuge.

And so it was that that fateful day, March 16, 2005 was one of utter terror, anticipation, frantic begging of top officials to lobby Senators and then despair and hopelessness, something I rarely feel with my inherit optimism. I was in my home town of Athens, Ohio, a nurturing and loving place for activists. After three months of near constant touring, I was taking a few weeks off, though certainly not off work to protect the great refuge.

It is fine to feel the utter horror and destruction that many of our politicians are pushing our planet toward. But we cannot let that steer us toward inaction. For me, organizing a presentation on

To Chad —
Best regards
Mike DeWine

The author, Kristine Kashmer of the Alaska Coalition, Ohio Republican Senator Mike DeWine and Chief Joe Linklater of Old Crow in Washington, DC, 2003.

the Arctic Refuge in my home town a week after the vote made me get too busy to despair, working in concert with my passion.

For years, various groups, from churches to hunting and fishing groups to environmental organizations of all kinds had set up and advertised my presentations all over the United States. But I wanted to just start organizing, to use the intense energy I felt for the great Arctic Refuge for something positive. I could set up the slide presentation in the public library meeting room for free, or on the College Campus with a student group's help. But there was a new community collective space, The Wire that was eager for more events, so I decided to hold it there.

I printed up a flier and made a sheet with 12 different panels giving the time, place and basics of the slide presentation. I printed fliers on color, reused paper, and the panels on reused paper (the back side of paper that was printed on one side that I no longer needed). I went to my favorite worker-owned restaurant/cantina, Casa Nueva and cut up the sheets with the 12 dupli-

Chad Kister, right, gives an award to Senator Michael DeWine in Columbus, Ohio, for the senator's vote to protect the coastal plain of the Arctic Refuge. Photo by Robert Kister, 2003.

cate panels into hand bills with scissors I carried in my backpack.

Then, I walked around, handing out hand bills, telling people about the event, and asking others to give out the hand-bills. With less than three dollars in printing costs and virtually no environmental impact, I had a packed room of people, and ready volunteers on a list for more action. If people around the country would begin to just start organizing, and working with established groups to do more and more events, we can protect the great Arctic Refuge.

Hold a slide or powerpoint presentation in your home town by one of the many people touring on this issue. Work with the Alaska Coalition (www.alaskacoalition.org), an unprecedented coalition of more than 900 religious, sporting, environmental and human rights organizations dedicated to protecting the Arctic Refuge, as well as other imperiled lands in Alaska. Show

one of the many DVDs or videos to groups, then have attendees
sign up on a sign up sheet and write letters to their Senators and
Representative. After enough people have been informed about
the Arctic Refuge, hold a rally or picket an Exxon station. Use
the mainstream media with press releases, public service
announcements and listings on calendars of events. Put up fliers
or posters and hand out handbills on reused or recycled paper.

It is up to us to see that the Arctic Refuge is to survive the
coming years. We do have power if we organize. This place is
just too important to let corporate President Bush destroy for
his oil cronies. There are times in our lives when we must make
sacrifices. Taking the sacrifice of time to organize and mobilize
politically is not only a very fulfilling endeavor, it is the only
chance we have left to save this most important area we have
for the survival of the last fully intact Arctic ecosystem with a
migrating caribou herd left in the world.

I have found that through activism, I could channel the
immense passion I have for saving this land into productive
education and political influence. I urge you as the reader to
invest more of your own time, in whatever means you can best
give to save this great refuge. There is a vast network of environmental organizations, undoubtedly many near where you
live. Coalitions can be formed locally to protect the Arctic
Refuge, or new groups created where none exist. Environmental
groups can join with social justice organizations because with
the Gwich'in people, this is very much a human-rights issue.
The Alaska Coalition can keep groups organized nationally.

After 30,000 years of living off the caribou, with wars
against neighboring tribes, diseases brought by white traders and
missionaries, the forced removal of their children from villages by
the state of Alaska and punishment of those who practiced native
traditions, the Gwich'in have never seen a threat greater to their
people and their sacred land than now. It is with great anger that
I listen on the radio to the oil industry financed Inupiat in native
corporations that would make millions of dollars from the

drilling, while the vast majority of native peoples who depend on the Arctic Refuge: the Gwich'in people are united in their opposition to drilling that would destroy their way of life.

And in fact, a majority of Inupiat in the village of Kaktovik—the only Inupiat village near the Arctic Refuge—signed a petition opposing oil development. And not everyone is willing to sign a petition, especially in such a small community. So undoubtedly a vast majority of the Inupiat peoples in Kaktovik are against the oil development. The Gwich'in, with 8,000 people who depend directly on the caribou whose nursery ground would be devastated by this development, are almost unanimously against destroying the coastal plain: the most sacred land of their people.

My extensive study of native peoples' opinions from my repeated travel throughout the region found that virtually all Gwich'in oppose drilling. Let's say 99 percent for purposes of this computation as my best estimate. With at least half of the 212 residents of Kaktovik also against it, that would mean 98 percent of the native peoples who live off the Arctic Refuge ecosystem oppose drilling. While this is by no means a scientific poll, the undisputed fact is that exponentially more native peoples in the region of the Arctic National Wildlife Refuge are strongly against drilling.

For national public radio and other media outlets to air only a native in favor of drilling, without countering it with one of the more than 95 percent of the native peoples in the Arctic Refuge region who oppose drilling is a dishonesty to the American people. Where were the Gwich'in voices in this debate? The media needs to keep reminding people that the vast majority of Americans and native peoples want the refuge protected, so they should include more people against drilling in their coverage to reflect that.

Again, we can make a difference. By writing letters to the editor, calling in to talk radio programs and organizing events or speakers and inviting local television and radio stations and newspapers, we can in our own ways in our home towns influence the media. We must not give up the fight. Even if drilling is passed in the budget, which looms before Congress in this April 2005 date, we will take it to court. For now, let's take this to the court houses of America with rallies and marches for the great Arctic Refuge.

It is the Gwich'in people, the last native people still living off a fully intact ecosystem left in the United States, whose fate we must protect. There is so much to learn from them that we do not know: about how to raise children to be gentle, understanding, intelligent and wise. We can learn how to live in harmony with Creation, and to not only respect but to religiously praise the animals, plants, land, water and air that feed and sustain them through ceremony and song.

After all we have done to nearly every corner of our globe; with 95 percent of the North Slope of Alaska already open to possible oil development; after our legacy of shame in our treatment of native peoples: can't we leave this one place and this one culture be?

This is a photo of some Gwichin youth in Old Crow in the Yukon Territories in Canada who depend upon the caribou that breed along the coastal plain in the Arctic Refuge.

About the Author

Born in Columbus, Ohio, Kister backpacked 700 miles from the oil fields of Prudhoe Bay into and throughout the Arctic National Wildlife Refuge in 1991, and published the book *Arctic Quest: Odyssey Through a Threatened Wilderness* about the journey. Kister has personally lobbied numerous U.S. Representatives and Senators to protect the refuge over the last 15 years. He has studied, written and spoken about climate change for nearly 20 years. In 2000, Kister was a climate campaigner with Ozone Action (now part of Greenpeace USA), and was a delegate to the United Nations Conference on Climate Change in the Hague, Netherlands in 2000.

For the last four years, Kister has traveled more than 40,000 miles through the United States and Canada, doing more than 500 slide presentations. Kister has traveled mostly by fuel-efficient train. In 2005, Kister joined the Board of Directors of the newly formed Arctic Voices organization, and was appointed vice-chair of the non-profit. Arctic Voices will strive to show the human face of the Arctic Refuge issue through the voices of the Gwich'in people.

Upcoming books by Kister include:

- "Against All Odds: The Struggle to Save Radar Hill," an inspiring narrative about the so-far success-

ful effort to protect the 700-acre Ridges nature preserve owned by Ohio University in Athens.

- a book about Kister's journeys through the Tongass
National Forest and southeast Alaska: the largest
old-growth forest in the United States. It is being
massively clearcut.

- a sequel to "Arctic Quest" about his journey from
Old Crow into the Arctic National Wildlife Refuge
in 2004.

Kister will return to the Arctic in the summer of 2005.

Color photos and maps of Kister's 700-mile journey
through the Arctic are at www.arcticrefuge.org where a CD
with high quality maps of the entire Arctic Refuge and hundreds of photos can be ordered. "Arctic Quest" and "Arctic
Melting" are also available on audio at www.chadkister.com.

He can be reached at www.chadkister.com or www.arcti-
crefuge.org.